COLLECTED POEMS

FREDA DOWNIE

Collected Poems

EDITED BY GEORGE SZIRTES

BLOODAXE BOOKS

ISBN: 1 85224 301 5

First published 1995 by
Bloodaxe Books Ltd,
P.O. Box 1SN,
Newcastle upon Tyne NE99 1SN.

Bloodaxe Books Ltd acknowledges
the financial assistance of Northern Arts.

Cover printing by J. Thomson Colour Printers Ltd, Glasgow.

Printed in Great Britain by
Cromwell Press Ltd, Broughton Gifford, Melksham, Wiltshire.

Contents

FORTY POEMS (1989)

INTRODUCTION

Freda Downie, who died on 5 May 1993, published relatively few poems in her lifetime: there were the two collections, *A Stranger Here* and *Plainsong*, published by Secker and Warburg in 1977 and 1981 respectively, a small clutch of pamphlets and some miscellaneous poems in magazines, anthologies and on competition lists. The two books were well received generally, and with particular enthusiasm by Geoffrey Grigson, but they did not climb to the top of the critical pile. If they did not make a big noise in the world it was because the clarity and precision of her poems seemed not to be striving for either largeness or clangour. There seemed to be no great technical innovation, no particular angle on the *zeitgeist* (the angle was on the universe rather than on any spirit of the age), no membership of any poetic party, no ostensible evidence of strident energy imposing complex shapes on the world. However – and it is an important however – the sheer purity of Downie's tone encompassed enough lights and darks to make an intense music of its own. It was a tone she hit relatively late in life, then held and maintained through almost everything she wrote. It is, I believe, a tone that will survive when many of the bigger noises of the world have faded away.

In assembling this volume, her husband David Turner has compiled a substantial number of uncollected poems from her papers, many of which I have added to the body of her published work. These range over some thirty years, the last twenty-six of which were spent in Berkhamsted. But Freda Downie, the poet, had been formed by experiences long before that. She was born in Woolwich on 20 October 1929. Her mother, Rose Dobinson, had had little formal education, having been kept at home to look after her younger sisters following the death of her father from blood poisoning. She worked at Tate and Lyle's sugar refinery and was pregnant with Freda when she married Cecil Downie. Downie, like Dobinson, was born in 1904. He was among the younger members of a family with ten children and little money. His parents had moved from Greenock in Scotland, his father being an engineering tradesman and violin teacher. The children were clever, energetic and musical. They became craftsmen, largely self-taught, in engineering and related trades, and could turn their hands to most of the types of work that came their way. Cecil Downie inherited these qualitities. His charm and skill on the piano made him popular at family gatherings but once married he exhibited an occasionally violent temper at home. He met Rose Dobinson when he too was employed by Tate and Lyle. They settled in Bexley.Heath and would go out cycling together on a tandem, the tiny Rose attempting to supplement Cecil's power at the pedals on the back seat.

Supplementing incomes was another matter. Freda Downie's first cradle was a drawer from a chest. Because of financial insecurity and Freda's obvious fragility, her mother ensured there would be no further children. Otherwise there was little mollycoddling. As soon as she was old enough the family would explore the Kent and Devon countryside on Cecil's Rudge Ulster motorbike with sidecar. Freda, not yet ten years old, was given an unusual amount of licence to roam, and walking in the country was to be her favourite method of relieving depression in later years. On the outbreak of war in September 1939 she was evacuated to Northamptonshire where she stayed with an 'uncle' and 'aunt' who had a son of their own, about a year older than her. There was also another boy, a fellow evacuee. The two boys gave Freda a very unhappy time until her mother's younger sister noticed things were not right and took her home where she spent the spring and summer. The family had no wireless and took no papers, so even with the Battle of Britain taking place over her head the course of the war was not well known to her. She had made close friends of a boy and girl with whom she played games of imagination. There were few books in the house. Her father played the piano though, and her first experience of poetry came from song lyrics such as: 'It was only a paper moon, hanging over a cardboard sea...'

The Blitz, when it came in September 1940, terrified and disturbed her. She could barely tolerate sudden or loud noises afterwards and was to suffer from nightmares throughout her life. In about September 1941, Cecil was offered an engineering job in Australia. Getting there entailed a long and dangerous journey by sea and he doubted the wisdom of undertaking it. Rose, however, argued that they could be killed just as easily if they stayed where they were and so, eventually, they decided to chance it. The experience of the three-month voyage out, the year and a half in Australia itself, and then the return journey, was to be one of the most vivid of Freda's life. Later she was to write it up and illustrate it with photographs (her journals and letters are all full of colour and delightfully written). It also established the cyclic pattern of her emotions, based on love, loss, depression and breakdown.

Her father's affair with another woman at this time effectively broke up the family. He stopped living with them and his financial support was sporadic. In 1946 he returned to Australia for another unsuccesful venture and Freda and her mother moved in with an aunt's family in South London. Freda left school, learned shorthand and typing, and began work at Novello's the music publishers in Wardour Street on a tiny salary. The compensation was the musical environment and the making of friends, a knack Freda kept throughout her life. Her lack of formal education left her with no sense of inferiority to anyone. But the job was repetitive and bored her; furthermore she was hopelessly in love with a boy she had met on the voyage back from Australia. He lived in North Shields and there was little chance of them meeting again (they managed it on one occasion) but they corresponded a great deal. Freda had become interested in Ancient Egypt and they shared this fascination, sending each other drawings of Egyptian ornaments, until Freda began to feel that Egypt meant bad luck. Later when David Turner gave her an Egyptian faience-ware necklace she rejected the gift and it was thrown away. The correspondence with the boy from North Shields lasted for three years, from 1944 to 1947. Her earliest efforts at poetry were contained in those letters.

Sometime in early 1950 Freda had her first nervous breakdown. By this time she and her mother were living in a flat in Elsham Road, W14, which her father, then working for the Medical Research Council, had managed to obtain for them. He turned up in their lives from time to time, occasionally violent then remorseful. Freda, on her part, hated giving way to anger and would always repress it as much as she could. She went to plays, exhibitions, concerts and films. She had started to learn the piano but in October 1951 her young piano teacher died suddenly, perpetuating the cycle of loss.

She had a succession of jobs, the most interesting of which was at James Bourlet, the art agents and framers. She sat in the main gallery and welcomed visitors such as Sir Thomas Beecham and Sir Oswald Birley. The woman in charge had taken a fancy to her and treated her like a protegé without giving her any serious responsibility. In August 1952 Freda suffered another breakdown and ran off to Dartmouth. She wrote in her journal: 'Am ill. No one can help. I cannot live, cannot sleep in London.'

In Dartmouth she made friends and was accommodated in a café by a kind Birmingham family, and enjoyed social life. Around Christmas her mother came to fetch her back.

Early in 1953 she started work at the Kingsway branch of W.H. Smith's library. This seems to be the time when she began reading with real consistency. The job at Bourlet's had been kept open for her and though she tried a brief return between June and November 1954 it didn't work out. She took a job in a florist's, then went back to the library, spending weekends away, out of London, as far as she could. In the October of that year she had received a letter from her first cousin, Bill, an engineer in Accra in Ghana. As a child in Devon he had thrown stones at her. Now he came to London on leave and together they visited Skye (which Freda associated with one of her favourite films, *I Know Where I'm Going*), a visit which was later to provide her with two poems, 'Miss Grant' and 'The Pleasure of Ruins', both printed in her second book, *Plainsong*. Soon he was proposing marriage, an offer which Freda eventually accepted, though she was unhappy about the closeness of the blood relationship, about Bill's character which was showing some likeness to her father's, about living in Africa and about the highly conventional marriage he would probably want from her. On the other hand he was handsome, charming, had connections in Devon, and took her to places she liked.

It was at this time she met David Turner, who was a member of Smith's library and alone in London. They got talking over books. She had approved his choice and they found they had many tastes in common. In July 1956 she suggested that they should visit the Picasso exhibition in St James's Square. As David Turner notes: 'Not bowled over by Picasso...but talked and talked in Green Park and were at ease.'

1956 was the decisive year. First she wrote to her cousin Bill, who was back in Africa by this time, cancelling the marriage (they were never to correspond again). In September Freda's father died suddenly, and in November, David Turner proposed, and she accepted. The Cold War, Suez, Hungary, and the first steps in space travel, all frightened her. She began to write seriously. She attended the City Lit for poetry appreciation and writing classes, and sent poems to Howard Sergeant's *Outposts* magazine (refusing to be tempted by publication at the cost of producing an Outposts booklet; she didn't appear in the magazine till 1961). On 29 March 1957 she and David Turner were married in Kensington Register Office and he moved in with her and her mother. Although the earning power of all three was low they would be able to combine their resources. Then Rose's lame Aunt Florence also moved in and remained till her death in 1959. Freda gave up the library and took on a succession of part-time jobs but didn't hold on to any of them for long. She had started, in her own words, 'to be domesticated'. David was transferred in October 1961, and the following February they moved to an old house in Buckingham town centre, taking Freda's mother with them. She was to stay with them to the end of her life in 1985.

Having moved to Buckingham, Freda missed London. She was isolated and could no longer get to the City Lit. However she did begin a correspondence of some thirty years with a fellow City Lit student, the poet Donald Ward. They sent each other poems for criticism, and a number of her uncollected typsecripts have his comments appended. This sustained her through bouts of depression and socialising. Pandora Hollander – the Pandora of 'Plainsong' – who was to commit suicide in Israel in 1970, became a close friend. *The New Republic* published two early poems of hers, 'A Bereavement' and 'The Bay'.

In June 1966 David was transferred to Stevenage, and they moved into a new development corporation house in the town. The change was a shock and a breakdown duly followed. Fortunately, David was transferred the following June to Hemel Hempstead and having sold the Buckingham house they found another in Berkhamsted.

In some ways, Freda's writing career began here. In the first place it was much simpler to visit the City Lit again, where the writing classes were now being led by Derek Stanford. Then in 1970 she won the Stroud Festival Poetry Competition with 'A Plain Girl', and a few years later met the poet and editor, John Cotton, who also lived in Berkhamsted. Fred Sedgwick, a younger poet arrived soon after. In fact there were a number of poets working in Hertfordshire during this period: Peter Scupham, John Gohorry, Roger Burford Mason and myself in Hitchin; John Mole in St Albans and Neil Powell in Baldock among others. Most of them were involved in the small press activity of the area. John Cotton had edited the magazine *Priapus*, which after the purchase of type from Oscar Mellor's Fantasy Press gave birth to the Priapus Press, still producing small booklets of poetry. In Hitchin The Cellar Press of the jazz musician John Myatt had spawned two further specialist poetry presses: Peter Scupham and John Mole's Mandeville Press and Roger Burford Mason's Dodman Press. Clarissa Upchurch and I set up The Starwheel Press to produce poems with etchings. Cellar, Mandeville, Dodman and Starwheel were at one time all operating from Hitchin. In St Albans the Ver Poets were (and still are) being run by May Ivimy. Freda's poems made the progress through most of these presses. Primarily on the basis of her first Mandeville and Priapus pamphlets, she was approached by Anthony Thwaite for Secker and Warburg, and in 1977 her first collection, *A Stranger Here,* was published.

On the surface Freda remained indifferent to publication. She was neither cowed by reputation nor envious of it. She certainly did not solicit it with any great energy, nor did she appear to keep particularly zealous track of reviews of her work. Equally, she showed no apparent distress when in 1986 Secker dropped her (as they did most of the poetry list). Having been reluctant to read in public, she felt she hadn't done much to help publicise her work and was therefore not entitled to complain if she was dropped. She had never owned to having written anything that might be called 'recently' but her output was now genuinely slowing down. A few private press collections continued to appear, and she was pleased to see her work being included in some anthologies, but the Hertfordshire poets began to break up. Fred Sedgwick moved away, then Peter Scupham, then Clarissa and I. Roger Burford Mason emigrated to Canada. In 1989 she submitted a set of *Forty Poems* to OUP. They were rejected.

The house in Berkhamsted had its disadvantages. It was dark and cold and had too many stairs. Her mother had died there. Having been stung by a bee she got a frozen shoulder which was only made worse by the chiropractor she consulted. She was no longer able to do the country walks which had been her salvation. She could no longer practice painting either, an activity that was perhaps dearer to her even than writing. She hated not being able to write. She often felt suicidal. In 1989 she developed a digestive problem. This was medically investigated but nothing specific was diagnosed. She was always an unlucky subject of medical treatment and did her best to avoid it. For a few more years she got along by avoiding certain foods and conserving her energy, but in March 1993 her nervous exhaustion and the digestive problem became acute and she took to her bed. She was unwilling to tolerate further medical investigation, saying, 'It would kill me.' After three weeks of almost no food and increasing exhaustion she reluctantly entered hospital where she soon suffered heart failure, from which she nearly died. Over the next five weeks her true condition remained obscure. Some underlying and dangerous fault in her blood chemistry was compounded and masked by a preoccupation with her history of neurosis. Taking hardly any food she drifted to her death which came on the 5th of May after pneumonia and final heart failure. Her last journal entry had been: 'Very cold – many murders, many road accidents – my sleeping habits, nightmares, worse than ever.'

*

It is very difficult to "place" Freda Downie's poetry. Her reading was essentially romantic: Keats, Hopkins, Poe, Dylan Thomas, Edith Sitwell and Virginia Woolf's *Orlando* were among her favourites. She adored the Americans, Elizabeth Bishop, Wallace Stevens, John Crowe Ransom and Hart Crane, and couldn't understand how a place which produced so many devices she hated and so much noise, could also produce such poets. She admired the novels of Patrick Hamilton and Jocelyn Brooke, and among her last loves were *Le Grand Meaulnes* and *Les Liaisons Dangereuses*. She read biography and history in intense phases, dictated partly by chance. She would buy books in the local library sale or at Oxfam and these would feed her imagination.

Painting excited her more than any other art form: David Jones, Rousseau, Modigliani, Soutine, Beckmann, Memlinc; and anonymous medieval manuscripts were particularly to her taste, as was the work of Paula Modersohn-Becker. She loved the painterly and the lyrical even in the more savage works of Beckmann and Soutine. In music her tastes ran to Ravel, Debussy, Fauré, Schubert and, above all, Chopin. The poets, painters and composers were whole people to her, victims of their biographies. Keats and Schumann were her 'poor old boys'.

Some of this might be guessed both from references in her poetry and from the very nature of it. Her painting owes something to Chagall, something to Gwen John, something to Lucien Freud, something to Modigliani and quite a lot to Modersohn-Becker. It is painterly, lyrical, often using conventional subjects – the portrait, the nude, flowers – in small but dense forms which, for all their intimacy and warmth of colour, have something intense and monumental about them. Her best work (what she thought of as her 'real paintings') certainly transcend the period feel.

In the same way her poetry exceeds the limitations implied by its apparently narrow range of symbols: moon, sea, painting, garden, empty room, lost friend or lover. There is little development once she finds her voice (perhaps a slight but inconsistent tendency to move away from rhyme) but the pitch, in her best poems, is perfect. *A Stranger Here* begins with 'Men without gardens':

Some men breathe evenly
In their illogical towers
Without knowing the name
Of the nearest flower shop
Or the short cut to the park.

The diction is almost colloquial but difficult to class, the transition from the symbolic 'illogical towers' to the commonplaces of flower shop and short cut to the park is managed simply, naturally, diminishing and undercutting the symbol. The even breathing locates the interior world easing us into the symbol that follows. There is a distant echo of Dorothy Parker's 'Chant for the dark hours' ('Some men, some men / Cannot pass a / Book shop') in the rhythm but Downie replaces her slightly nagging, bitter-sweet lilt, so easily parodied, with something more four-square yet brittle.

Others move slowly
Over acres of dry carpet –
Like snails who inadvertently
Enter back kitchens –
Hang curtains of leaves
At blank windows
And pant in verandah jungles,
Dreaming a voice calls them in
From a ground-floor window.

Both types of men are vulnerable dreamers and the usually prosaic device of a simile leads here to a full development invoking domestic reality (snails entering 'back kitchens'), some Douanier Rousseau-ish exoticism ('pant in verandah jungles') and a kind of empty illusionistic terror ('curtains of leaves / At blank windows'). Illogical towers are offered as the antithesis of blank windows but neither offers much fulfilment. The voice that calls 'From a ground-floor window' is both welcoming and admonitory. It may belong to mother or to death. Flower shop, park, curtains of leaves and verandah jungles are elements of the restricted and domesticated nature from which both men are separated. The lightness of tone in which the parable-like comparison is delivered carries a sense of certainty. The poet feels pity for her creatures but hovers above them, herself trapped at blank windows and illogical towers. That maternal voice is not so much hers as that of some kind of alternative – or Anti-Nature – sensible, desirable yet terminal.

. These men are cousins to Elizabeth Bishop's manmoth. The poet knows them better than they do themselves. She would know the way to the flower shop, she would realise the tower is illogical, she would observe the snails entering her back kitchen and know that men look out of blank windows, but nature lies beyond her too. The voice that calls them calls her.

The poem's easy manner, its domestic terms of reference, its very neatness might suggest something minor and conventional to a perfunctory or agenda-seeking reader, but Downie's politics are complex and her precision is authoritative. Her attention is not distracted by the processes of her own imagery. The gentle sounding poem is taut with its freight of pity and foreboding. Whoever is dispensing "wisdom" from on high is walking her own tightrope.

The politics are complex because Downie's were instinctive and elusive. She had little faith in practical politics: nothing could be achieved by any -ism, whether this be socialism, toryism or feminism. Such things made her angry. They were missing the point. The trick was to see people in the round and to understand their – and the poet's own – distress. But one had to achieve this with tact, without egotism, without drawing attention to the melodramatic self. She was a sublimator, not a confessor.

Only occasionally does she venture into autobiography. In the title poem of her first book gardens and dreams re-appear. 'Trees and hills hold their greens at one remove / Like false properties of hot dreams. /...My veins are taut, run green, and stretch / To a perimeter, described by leaves. /...Rain drops, heavy as a cat from a table...' The poem ends:

A boy on a tractor pulls his duffel hood
Against nails of rain hammered to the ground,
A sow escapes the measure of her freedom

And frantic men chase the pink hullabaloo.
I did not wait for this, but this will do.
Someone lights a window to make sure of things.
('A Stranger Here')

The penultimate line is absolutely Downie. It is the resigned, ironic but firm voice accepting the brief pink conflagration, the moment of freedom, but seeing it from the outside, and seeing, equally, the boy hammered by the rain, at the very moment when she seems to have become part of nature.

The terms of the drama remain very similar throughout Downie's poetry, in fact one might argue it is the same drama only the actors and the setting varying, but its scope increases as the incidents multiply. 'In the House', a poem from *Plainsong*, pictures a man dying. His wife brings him a flower from the garden, 'Saying, *Look it is open this far. /* And the man regards the powdery star. / Later, the woman leaves the house again / And returns with another flower / Saying, *Now it is open this far* '. Nature paces out the distance to death, keeping it on a tight leash. Nature is exemplary, beautiful and indifferent. Its very delicacy is cutting. 'Plainsong', the title poem addressed to the dead Pandora Hollander, begins ceremoniously:

> I am like that bereaved emperor
> Longing for his lovely lady,
> But I would not crook a finger
> At courteous magicians or
> Cry out at shadowy conjurations.

The language is lightly pitched up, nodding to John Crowe Ransom ('For I must have my lovely lady soon' from *Piazza Piece*), its manners slightly arch: emperors, ladies, crooked fingers, magicians. Death is approached as a piece of stage magic, fully in character. It is a formalised world of 'kind fraudulence', where the poet now wearing 'rain on plain sleeves' no longer looks for

> the reality
> Of your inattentive face
> In the shadows of old photographs
> Where you sit in ancient gardens
> With an averted gaze, or
> At café tables wearing dark glasses.

There are masks for everything. The garden is ancient: the friend a mystery. The language has turned as plain as her sleeves (but one does think of conjuror's sleeves too). The truth,

> Is an uncertainty, a turning away –
> And no dark parlour conjuring
> Would prove your many departures
> Were not of your own choosing.

One behaves well, in other words, but one knows it is only a trick, that the disappearance was for real and always intended.

The archness is part of the poetry. In life it could be infuriating but one sensed the plain sleeves underneath and knew it to be important. It carried its own irony with it. The bereaved emperor with his crooked finger had to be kept in view and his lovely lady always to be desired. Power and traditional enchantments were all too likely to be conjuring tricks and could be magicked away. Nevertheless emperors are emperors and Freda never forgot she was one, even if only by the conjuring trick of language: the lovely lady was always to be calling the emperor through the ground floor window.

20

One may usefully think of the poems as a single drama of confrontation with the tragic muse. Downie was in many ways a muse poet in the Gravesian sense. She could describe the goddess and continually presented her magical island. She also knew the goddess was dangerous: that she fed – to be absolutely plain about it – on her depressions. At the same time it was important that the goddess be confronted, that one's tragic mask should not be ridiculous; that it was only right that it should have a slightly arch expression because this made the mask human. She hated bombast and rhetoric, what she referred to as the 'I, I, I...me, me, me' of more strident poets. Hating this was one with hating the terrible loud noises of the Blitz or the furies of her father. But the mask was never comfortable. As Wallace Stevens said, it was to be 'strange, however like'. There is nothing comfortable about any of this. The neatness of the poems is not cosy: the individual, apparently modest and neat poems add up to an oeuvre that continually deepens the tragic myth on which they depend.

Among her last poems we find 'Window', 'Yes' and 'Like Kylerhea'. The sea is now the central symbol. In 'Window', a boy is 'playing with the lonely sea' as the dusk advances while

> houses look to themselves,
> Look blindly away from the darkening game
> In which the boy runs purposefully
> Seawards and shorewards at the tide's edge
> Like someone bearing a message no one
> Wishes to receive – something written long ago
> In his head, now overgrown with hair.
> He will never stop running, for his limbs
> Are oiled, his skill increases mysteriously
> And the sea has become hopelessly attached.

The sea 'rushes after him, monstrously grey; / But when he turns it whitens and retreats'. Inside the house 'Someone very quietly plays Reynaldo Hahn' but the boy does not know this, 'he is turning and running again / To hidden music, as if for the first time.'

The boy is sacrificially oiled. It is the sea that has him on a string. 'Soon the game must end unaccompanied.' The extraordinary depths of this poem in which one reads the quiet music in the house both as counterpoint and premonition depends on the poet's understanding of the sea as something that may be played with (the boy is only human, he pretends the sea is retreating from him) but which will exact its due recompense. The great archetypes of sea, youth and house are brought down to an act of naming: Reynaldo Hahn. It is like the cry of Rilke for Gaspara

Stampa in the *First Duino Elegy*. Ideas and sensations are focused and made human.

'Window' is a very large poem. Much shorter, 'Yes' recalls Bede in the flight of the sparrow through the house, then provides another image for transience: 'a stone thrown at the sky-reflecting ocean / That bounces once, with a fountain-splash, before sinking'. The second verse turns this into a love poem with the single memory of meeting a 'winsome dog…down an empty lane / That charged you from an unfenced garden, happily growling, / Its muzzle a black gloss clenched on a stone, / Knowing you alone would amuse, for ever – in passing'. The poem only has ten lines. Here is the sea, here is the garden, here is affection and nature bounding at you, the lane empty. Dog and sea are superimposed on each other, and the 'certain' love, of which the poem speaks is thrown into long perspective.

'Like Kylerhea' was the poem read after her funeral. It begins in her chatty tone, with images of the ferryman who is to carry her across to the land of the dead. He is a real ferryman, but there is something childish, emblematic in his 'blue woollen hat, a striped jersey / And canary-coloured waterproofs'. He is not to be dressed portentously, no Dantesque Charon. Her funeral cortege is to be 'easy seals' that 'rise / To the occasion of my passing / In their best black'. Even the seals shall maintain their manners, their black not that of nature but of an outfit adopted with no more or less self-consciousness than would be accepted of such civilised creatures. Their very archness is easy. The poem ends:

> I want nothing of the far side,
> Other than what is already there;
> And when the ferryman says
> 'Nothing lasts for ever',
> I shall want to believe him.

This is marvellous poetry: understated, tragic, wholly human, not one word affected. The ferryman and the seals have already been set up and it needs only the plainest of language to tap their terrible power. 'Other than what is already there' seems almost not to be line of poetry at all but its effect is deep as any funeral bell.

Beside the *Forty Poems* submitted to OUP, all included here, Freda Downie left behind almost two hundred uncollected poems from which I have selected sixty-six. Mostly, these were poems Freda either failed to publish or decided against publishing. I chose them because they seemed good poems to me, poems interesting in their own right and important in fleshing out that sense of an *œuvre* which I believe is central to any just evaluation of her work. It was hard to date them very accurately, particularly because, as I have already mentioned, there are few stylistic grounds available on which to posit a development as such. David Tumer has, however, managed to sort them into groups by reference to specific places or events. There are a couple of poems from the late fifties, a few more from the Buckingham period between 1962 and 1966, some from the late 60s, and others which could be dated only as early, mid or late 70s, or simply 70s. There are a few from the 80s and then the last poems at the end of the collection. I have not thought it important to place each poem in its first publication, though these were available in some cases.

In doing so I am all too aware how great my debt is to David Turner. Nothing of this could have been done without him. In life it was he who undertook the task of supporting Freda: most of the business of daily routine and survival after his retirement was down to him. His sensitivity and intelligence sustained and complemented hers. His labour in collecting, sorting and providing reference points for the poems and the biographical part of this introduction has made my task the relatively simple one of selection and presentation.

This volume of Freda Downie's *Collected Poems* aims to provide a rounded picture, not a comprehensive one. It also wants to make certain claims for her. It wishes to suggest that she was a far more important poet than people thought: not in the sense that she begat schools or imitators (she was not an "influence" as Eng Lit understands the term) but in that she was an extraordinarily "real" poet, to use her own term of approbation, one whose work has a clarity available only to a few writers. Paradoxically, this is precisely what makes her work available to a wide range of readers. She is a myth-maker and myth-enacter on a human scale. Her world is one of universals humanly perceived through sad minutiae but the sea that she invokes is melancholy and brooding in the full Romantic manner. Her poems belong, if one has to "place" them anywhere, with the Dickinson heritage of power through limit. Their manners are wholly English but their apprehensions are stateless.

Beside David Turner, particular thanks are also due to Donald Ward, John Cotton, Peter Scupham and John Mole who have supported and believed in her work and greatly helped mine. I feel very much a junior partner to all of them.

GEORGE SZIRTES

ACKNOWLEDGEMENTS

The edition includes all the poems in Freda Downie's two book-length collections, *A Stranger Here* (1977) and *Plainsong* (1981), both originally published by Secker & Warburg, as well as the whole of her unpublished collection *Forty Poems* (1989). Several poems in those collections first appeared in small press publications: *Night Music* (The Mandeville Press, 1974); *A Sensation: Cellar Press Poems 18*, illustrated by Mary Norman (The Cellar Press, 1975); *Night Sucks Me In* (Priapus Press, 1976); *A Berkhamsted Three*, with Fred Sedgwick and John Cotton (Priapus Press, 1978); *A Starwheel Portfolio*, with John Gohorry and John Mole, with etchings by Clarissa Upchurch, George Szirtes and Paul Martin (The Starwheel Press, 1978); *Man Dancing with the Moon* (The Mandeville Press, 1979); and *Even the Flowers* (Gruffyground Press, 1989). Other poems appeared in various Mandeville Press anthologies, including *Nine Muses 2* (1975), *A Mandeville Fifteen* (1976), *Spring Collection* (1977), *Winter Dragoncards* (1978), *Mandeville's Travellers* (1984), *A Mandeville Bestiary* (1985) and *Home Truths* (1987).

Acknowledgements are also due to the editors of the following publications in which poems from *Forty Poems* first appeared: *Encounter, First and Always: Poems for Great Ormond Street Children's Hospital* (Faber, 1988), *The Rialto* and *Slipping Glimpses* (Poetry Book Society Supplement, 1985), and to BBC Radio 3 for 'While the Sun Shines', 'Ship in a Bottle' and 'Invitations to Voyage with Mr Alfred Wallis', which were first read on *Poetry Now*. Only two poems in the *Uncollected Poems* section have been previously published: 'Window' in *Even the Flowers* (Gruffyground Press, 1989) and 'Like Kylerhea' in *Vision On* (Ver Poets Anthology, 1992).

A STRANGER HERE

(1977)

Men without gardens

Some men breathe evenly
In their illogical towers
Without knowing the name
Of the nearest flower shop
Or the short cut to the park.

Others move slowly
Over acres of dry carpet –
Like snails who inadvertently
Enter back kitchens –
Hang curtains of leaves
At blank windows
And pant in verandah jungles,
Dreaming a voice calls them in
From a ground-floor window.

Our Loves

The poets who never grow old –
They are one of our many loves.
It is as if their drownings,
Their suicides and interminable coughing
Are just so much more poetry
Completing something unfinished in ourselves.

How long it takes –
The cultivation of formal laurels –
And when we come across a photograph
Of an enlarged poet prospering in a warm climate,
Unrecognisable in a hat and whiskers,
What inescapable prose confronts us.

For Wilfred Owen

Today you would find your distant sad shire
Apparently forgetful of slaughtered innocence
And given wholly to the business of spring.
If you were to approach Habberley for instance,

By way of the stream and erratic plovers,
You would meet a girl in a dedicated mood
Airing the newest generation in a pram
While carefully avoiding the lane's yeasty mud.

And later, the village dog would confront you
With his oddity of one grey eye and one brown
Dancing attendance on your singularity,
Until you stopped by a cottage almost overgrown

With the season and the gardener's art,
Where even the doorway frames an affair
Of flowers fuming in an old tin helmet
Resigned to being always suspended there.

On the Estuary

This is the poet's house, pushed well out to sea.
Here all the children of his fathering
Moved to the laws of his astonishing music
And here he wrote in his head all night long,
Where now rooms bang with emptiness all night long
Like old cannons puffing and blowing down the coastline.

It seems soon the abandoned house may lose its footing
And slip into the sea, or the sea may slip into the house
When fish, cold as death and with salt in their eyes,
Would move from room to room with depressive mouths
Reading nothing at all into neglected masonry.

But so far the house has kept its feet dry
Between the colours of the sea and the colours of the wood
And the raven still clears its throat to say nothing but
Oak leaves and sticks, oak leaves and sticks,
While the owl remains dry and derisive
And the shored heron maintains
Unalterable attitudes before flight
Can appear impressive in retrospect.

Light too remains impervious and endurable,
Nosing repeatedly around the blank walls;
But it is not the light of the mind revealing
Lines finer than fine writing.
It is the light of one more morning and one more morning
That would, without being asked,
Show someone entrenching tools –
Someone who knows how to hang a blue plaque
And how to order slim blue volumes from the mainland.

Night Music

A little night music Mr Mozart if you please.
I have folded the newspaper and put Asia to bed.
Knives are scraping plates in the next room
But penury still turns her seams.
A little night music Mr Mozart if you please.

All I know is the revolution of my gramophone
And the compulsion of your frilled wrists.

I am sorry only snow attended your funeral.
I am sorry I was not there.
Mr Mozart, a little night music if you please.

Shell

When his starched attendant leaves him,
He takes the sea-shell from the shelf
To hold, as though he were Orpheus holding
The possibility of music to himself.

And where once he heard uninterrupted guns
And the saturation of drowning fear,
He now discerns a hushed and calmer issue when,
Trembling, he holds the shell against his ear.

He has waited long to hear pacific waters
And the wind calling him across wet sands.
O now, now he can sleep and let the veins
Run sea-blue and cold in his submissive hands.

Running Boys

Desultory sun reappears
To lick the sombre grass lazily,
Pucker the face of the pallid pond
And play on the soundless floor
Beneath the oriental gestures
Of the bandstand's turquoise canopy.

And beyond the silent memorial
To summer's hot raspberry music,
Bright running boys wearing red jumpers
Thread warmth through despondent trees,
Hunting the winter heart more swiftly
Than Uccello's cardinal riders
Negotiating the endless wood.

Some Poetry

Poetry is a loose term and only
A fool would offer a definition.
Those not concerned with the form
At all usually refer to some
Beautiful manifestation or the other.

Chopin, dying in hellish foggy London,
Wrote to say he was leaving for
Paris to finish the ultimate act,
Begging Grzymala to make his room ready
And not to forget a bunch of violets
So that he would have a little poetry
Around him when he returned.

I like to think the violets were
Easily obtainable and that the poetry
Was there, on the table, breathing
Wordless volumes for one too tired
To turn pages while moving swiftly
Towards an inevitable incomprehensible form.

Orpheus is walking

Orpheus is walking through the wood,
His lyre grown heavy, his sandal thongs gone slack.
The trees thin and the arterial road arrives
Conveying the progressive automobile,
But he does not care for such discordance
Or the tenor of automatic horns.

The delicate mauves of his eyelids droop
And his sighs lift the leaves of the trees.
He turns a torn heel and goes slowly back.

A Lesson

When the boy entered the room again,
The size of the piano overwhelmed him
And the chair seemed an impossible throne
From which he must rule dissenting time.

And when he sat down to play intensely,
The simplest piece fractured beneath his hands
While the clacking metronome persistently
Rang out the intervals of urgent demands.

He thought time conspired with his tutor,
But he could not comprehend the part she played
Or see how time had so much altered her
From the portrait of her earlier head

And when she turned away to mark his music,
He sighed and looked to the window to see
His bicycle gleaming in the early dusk
Against the rain-wet trunk of the apple tree.

Great-grandfather

Great-grandfather would sit in the back parlour
For hours listening to the gramophone.
I have no photograph of him doing this,
So the picture I see of him sitting alone

With his head inclined towards the trumpeting
Green lily is colourful and unfaded.
The handkerchief, with which he blots the tears
Schubert serenades from him, is distinctly red

And the gramophone's tin horn grows steadily
More greenly lily-like and rare,
Grows into antiquity – and soon will be found
Surviving only behind glass in conditioned air.

Great-grandfather knows nothing of this, but
Such an instrument will be treasured as though
It were a silver trumpet once discovered
Lying in the tomb of some young Egyptian Pharaoh;

And only on certain occasions will it be taken
From its case and played with careful ceremony –
When thinnest sound will summon the ready armies
Of imagination to salute the music lovers of history.

And great-grandfather will be one of those.

Her Garden

My grandmother grew tiny grapes and tiger-lilies,
But there is no sentimental cut to her garden
Through a fat album or remembered lane;
Only interior voyages made on London ferries

Paddling the Thames' wicked brew to Silvertown,
Where regular as boot boys, the factories
Blacked her house every day, obscured the skies
And the town's sweet name at the railway station.

Between ships parked at the end of the road
And factory gates, she kept her home against soot,
Kept her garden colours in spite of it –
Five square feet of bitterness in a paved yard

Turned to the silent flowering of her will,
Loaded with dusty beauty and natural odours,
Cinnamon lilies, and the vine roots hanging grapes,
Sour as social justice, on the wash-house wall.

The Poor

The poor are still standing in the snow
Announcing their silence with cracked lips.
They do not move or go away
And time unravels their gloves.

When the snow ceases to flurry,
Winter Palaces sweeten the distance
Reflecting the sun with a million windows.
But the decorated doors remain closed.

No one comes in wide sleeves
Carrying hot wine in a jade cup.
No one comes in thick uniform
Bearing rough blankets.

Swan Song

Sometimes the sameness of swans overwhelms me.
I can never look at one for long without seeing
The swan someone photographed in the park years ago.
The swan stands on the far side of a low railing
Close to my father, who stands this side of the railing.
They are both carefully posed and in fine feather.
My father holds his cigarette no less elegantly
Than the swan holds its neck – but it is obvious
Only strategic fencing keeps them together –

And my father has one hand in his pocket
As though he, too, were unacquainted with base emotion
And incapable of sudden flight.

When

When you finally give up abstraction,
You will start a new school of realism
And people will crowd the gallery
To admire your painting
Of a woodland green with winter
Where snow falls continually, meltingly,
Between mossy columns on to
Separate blades of grass.
Ah, they will say, discerningly,
But still he only handles silence.
The movement is the wind's discretion.

And when your table groaningly resigns
Under the weight of commissions
And you find you can no longer
Delineate the recession of a wave
Or the downfall of tears with any passion,
You will enter a new dimension altogether
That will confound the gilders and framers
And leave your severest critic
With nothing to consult but his watch.

The Burning Babe

(after Robert Southwell)

The other night I saw a burning Babe,
But it was no vision of holiness.
Its passion was the anguish of a child –
Not the passion of some enduring god –
And the darkness of its mouth opened wide
Crying *I am not on fire to work your good.*
I fled Hell's tongues, but they will have their say;
I burn that men may live only as they choose.
My skin is taken, yet none will put it on.
My name is Asia and tears dry at my heat.

And straight I called to mind, that day
Was not marked holy or significant.

O Mary

O Mary
The girls in the convent
Are performing Die Fledermaus tonight.
Their faces are painted as beautifully as yours
And their borrowed dress is as long as yours.
They are very excited, but you remain calm
With your dolly blue glass eyes turned to God
In the solid resignation of your unmoving face.
It is the interval now and they decorate doorways.
The red headed girl in the black cape and top hat
Is handsome enough to escort me around the dusk
Of the damp grounds and empty swimming pool,
But she is very popular.
And Mary,
Although they promenade beyond the delicate
Blue light cast about you by a glass cupola heaven,
They appear to bear a life as charmed as your own.

Meister Bertram 1345-1415

The candid commentaries caress.
Fluent Christ, red robed, gestures gently
And a whole menagerie is blessed.
Stiff peacocks respond, bears and foxes
Show teeth inconsequentially
For laughter and wolves love sheep dearly.

Then red robed again, on a shrewd ass,
Sadly entering Jerusalem
And adored by devout gentlemen,
While others hurrah Him with wrong leaves,
Or show stylish legs in smart blue hose
From a good view in intricate trees.

These exquisite errors find Him.
All mine, less bright, leave me where I am.

A View

Snow fills the square this fine morning
Masking the features of the fountain statue.
Pigeons worry the careful blue shadows
And religion parades the square this morning.

Here are two handmaids of God in dark habits
And linen hats prepared for pure flight.

And here comes God Himself with a priest and boy –
A last sacrament in a small receptacle hurrying
To someone declining from the fineness of the morning.

The Italians Are Excited

The Italians are excited.
They keep standing up to look out of the train.
Spring sunshine ripens their hands and accents,
Spring sunshine colours winter trees and rubbish.
They cannot be admiring the landscape, yet one would think
They were just entering the Ticino and passing the first vineyard.
They keep standing up to look over the head of the driver.
They must be gauging the advancing complexity of rails
Or the Englishness of English overhead wiring.
They are not interested in the driver
Or the sun yellowing their hands.

Only when the train nears the city station
Do they empty their eyes and sit down in silence.

Christmas

Christmas in the parlour revolving under
A heaven of paper constellations,
Curtained with lace starched to the sharpness
Of frost flowers drawn against the night.
Aunts and uncles expanding the square root
Of one torrid room with their new looks
Radiating beneath regal and rakish angles
Of tissue hats, and the salt of their tears
Coursing to the ritual of sentimental tunes,
Carnival novelties and inspired lunacy.
The chiffonier insisting on a merry Christmas
In every shaped mirror and coldly repeating
Piled fruit and happiness for ever.

Enduring colours of happiness and cut paper,
Portable as Victorian paper-weights.

O the sombre fingers of the little tree
And glassy darkness of aspidistras
Smoothing hot frivolity and loss.

Carol

       O Lord we wait.
The Brick Company owns many fields
Where chimneys create new horizons
And the Air Ministry commands many fields,
Dismantling our roof with explosive fuels.
       And Lord, we wait.

       O Lord we wait.
Our fields between freeze in dark anonymity.
One star is dislodged and chalks black heaven.
It is a dissolution and anonymity.
It is not a steady shining presence.
       Yet Lord, we wait.

       O Lord we wait.
Our outbuildings are soft with straw.
In one barn there is bitumen, an old coat
And a bicycle only. The manger spills straw,
The floor also – and there is room for three.
       And Lord, we wait.

The Bay

I should like to think the purple flowers on the
Green cliff and the purple patching the bay below
And this hot lizard, indicate the finer points
And threads of some intricate pattern; but I know
Minute maps of purple on a momentary spine
Do not emulate nameless places of the sea;
And that tiny boat there is not rocking on an
Armful of jewels, but proceeds with audacity
Across the cold arena like a butterfly
Moving over the green gravel of a formal grave.
And all that is more than meets the eye, looms with
Dead certainty beneath each perfunctory wave,
While the occupants of that tiny boat cast out
Their hopes, and knowing the balm of occupation,
Drag abundant sustenance from the wet charnel
Of lives and voyages lost in dark inundation.

I should like to think some supernatural note
Will sound, resurrecting the better part of men,
When historical and unrecorded navigators
Will surface, joyful as seals and unforgotten,
The flesh and flash of salty eyes restated.
But I know the flimsiest spirits do not rise
Like evaporating rain on the lighthouse path.
Only evaporating rain ascends to warmer skies
In ghostly columns – and where this path ends
The lighthouse waits to flail wild arms into the night,
Rescuing no one and merely indicating
Protruding rocks and death with efficient light.

Railway Butterfly

Early sun rivets you to the station wall
And flattens your colours on the platform,
But should you desire anything at all
Beyond the warmth of this gritty place,
You will learn honey is never shunted here.

Perhaps you are that thoughtful gentleman
With more than time enough to spare
Dreaming he is, without doubt, a butterfly;
In which case, this dry suspension
Will be acceptable enough.

But, if you are that frail proposition
Dreaming you are a philosopher,
Then, like me, you cannot be unaware
Of aridity's interminable dimensions
Entering the questionable dream we share.

Invocation

Come Rousseau,
The moon is consequential tonight.
Twice, since you put down your brush,
The park has filled with soldiery,
But you would find the place recognisable again.
The empty bandstand still wears its steady crown
Prolonging a silent music
And the damp grass bends its perfume.

Come Rousseau,
The moon cuts her careful silhouettes
And the names of Harlequin and Columbine
Are not entirely forgotten.

Emperor Chi'en-lung on Horseback

(a painting on silk in the Kyoto Museum, Japan)

The Emperor Chi'en-lung, wearing a modest
Cinnamon coloured robe and a black hat,
Is in the spring meadow inspecting his horses.
He himself is mounted on a faultlessly accoutred
High horse that requires only admiration
And he has turned the pallor of his face to his attendant,
Who stands deferentially at his side wearing
A similar robe the colour of turned sheepskin
Or pale quince. He also wears a black hat
Apparently indistinguishable from the emperor's.

They are standing near a leafless willow tree
And the willow tree is standing near a tiny tree
That arranges atmosphere with ethereal pink blossom.
And beyond all this, the meadow's light spreads;
But it is difficult to determine the nature
Of the effulgence and the early weather.
The whiteness of snow, or frost perhaps, is blown
On the willow's trunk, but the willow's bare branches
Drop effortless green lines like spring rain,
And the meadow, stretching further than the eye can see,
Seems to be a sheer sheet of glassy ice or snow,
When it does not appear to be an arena of warm spring mist
Or some floor of celestial light even.

Perhaps it is, after all, merely delineation
Of celestial light – for landscapes of seasonal light
Shared by two solitary figures, with or without horses,
Are more than rare.

And the horses. Where are the emperor's horses?
They are nowhere to be seen – unless they are
Here, in front of the emperor, warming our sides
With the history of their resilient flanks.

Ikon

The king of that country, when he died,
Turned sideways, leaning his head
Against a peerless blue until
The colour of heaven became indisputable
About the gravity of his heavy crown –
And the significance of his features
Reared monumentally kind.

And the king of that country, when he died,
Grasped in the wealth of his hand,
An astonishingly small flower
Wrought of natural petals on a stem –
Modest as a weed in a ploughed furrow,
Scarlet as blood replenishing a furrow.

Horse-sense

The untarnishable features of Charlemagne
Bestride the progress of the little horse.
Clever horse, to bear the unevenly
Distributed burden of kingship.
How neatly he can turn the sharp corners
Of battlefields and with what consideration
He drops his forelock to the Pope.
With his right foreleg he can tap out
The number of miles to Babylon from anywhere
And even Jerusalem would acclaim
The modest music of his accoutrement.

Clip, clip, go his precise hooves
As he picks his way steadily
Through the leaves of books.
Clip, clip, go his hooves
As he trots fastidiously
Between the words of endless sentences.

Horoscope

Come, look at this bright powder
Devoid of scintillating implications.

The stars foretell
Nothing but their infinite indifference.

See how well they keep their distance
For substantial charting – unless we stoop

To disturb their vain repetitions
In the blackness of near water.

You

You shape your lips,
Stand whistling at the moon
And rattle small change
In the linen of your pocket.

The moon shaped her lips long ago –
But nothing came of it.
She is above sistrums and flutings
And will never come to observe
The dark places in your whitened head.

Funny Man

The cat looks at the king
and the wag in the pied suit
shakes his metallic bells, pokes
an obscene tongue in open spaces,
yet keeps his insolent head.

Come then, in black and white
or in your saucy flesh, for
unanswered petitions leave me
confounded and with a royal need
for hilarious attendance.

Gesture broadly on the pier,
crack your red lips everywhere
until acclaiming hand clap
to emulate doves returning
with individual green sprigs.

Or simply tumble down.
This is my hoop stretched
with delicate paper, busy
with a nimbus of dramatic
and self-consuming flames.

Perform.

How Easily

How easily it alters the air
And drifts through the stations–
Of unprotesting trees

And when it comes to the garden,
What a strict line it observes
At the window's light

As though the wrist's movement
Or the least flick of will
Would prove brilliant annihilation,

As though it would doff a hat
Before entering doors
Or the spaces of pillowed heads.

Moon

Let alone the moon
Preserving her pocked face.
I have been over familiar
With her pitiless stare and know
She uses arsenic to whiten her hands.

How she eats my flesh.
How she disregards my bones
While bleaching them.

Mountain Road

I contract to a heart beat.
It is not a swung lantern suddenly explaining
The shape of black trees, but the summer moon.

It is an absurd size,
Swollen with light and floating out of orbit,
Capable of eclipsing the entire night.
It is not a disc to reckon with, a nursery moon
Drawn or pasted at a reasonable distance.
The old man has gone and only mountains remain,
Ranged impersonal heaps shadowing moon and earth.

Unable to match thought with this immensity,
My feet flounder on the earth's steep sides

And scuttling, I descend
To a different prospect of twilight sea
Where a dreary light flattens the water's rim,
Hopeless as the framed gloom of a sleepless night.
The shore rocks are black as death, are meaningless,
And livid clouds narrowing the light
Hang level with me, weathered to a vision
Of enormous hands, supernatural and waiting.

The grey grass at my feet
Smells sweeter than it did at noon, but I want
A room of easy dimensions and words to answer.

A Stranger Here

Silence thickens, muffling the stuffy landscape.
Trees and hills hold their greens at one remove
Like false properties of hot dreams.

Grey skies oppress the rim of the woods
And not one song is unravelled from the sickness
Of garlic flowers in fissured darkness.

My veins are taut, run green, and stretch
To a perimeter described by leaves.
I wait, every detail waits
For something – for someone recognisable
Approaching with special lotions and explanations.

Rain drops, heavy as a cat from a table,
Shaking the composure of a broad leaf.
Time recants and I turn a quiet corner.

A boy on a tractor pulls his duffel hood
Against nails of rain hammered to the ground,
A sow escapes the measure of her freedom

And frantic men chase the pink hullabaloo.
I did not wait for this, but this will do.
Someone lights a window to make sure of things.

The Watercolourist

Not the conflagration of distant cities,
But merely the question of the sun
Going, or coming perhaps, beyond trees.
And the trees, always the extent of trees
With their total sum of countless leaves
And footpaths halting at formal waters.

No, no one emerges large as life from this
Dividing the trees with a solitary grief
Or spilling vitriol from a shadowed mouth
And no one fulfils foregrounds to climb their
Smiling over rigid frameworks of park railings –
For all the paths coming and going arrive
At nothing more than more bosky distances,
Hazardless and uninhabited but for
Passionless gestures of concealed statuary.

Yet he would, oh if there were talent,
Discreetly adhere to each landscape
Tentative semblances of reticent lives
Spent at a distance and always sideways on,
As though sharing a dream with Corot.

Or with one leap, he would arrive at
The mastery of art, reassembling
Heavenly pinks and skeletal darks until
He arrived at one perfect unquestionable form.

Conjuror

Night suited him perfectly
With dark tailoring
When he drew, not from his rib,
But from the cuff of his secret sleeve,
Streaming silks of her pure form.
Then, with what legerdemain
The silk of her flesh assembled
And slowly turned towards him
To a sound of immanent doves
And how the solitary rose of her mouth
Widened when she moved forever forward
With a trump card blazing in her hand
To tensions preparing a final chord

Until he cried
At the protraction of her nearness
And conjuration of her secrets,
Soft as concealed conies,
And shook his brief wand
At morning's appearance
Bearing all the birds beyond his jurisdiction.

The Topiarist

Imperceptibly his art has hedged him in
With the company of pampered shapes
And you are hedged out with bosky formality.
No, he has no room for riotous beds
Or the cold fixity of statues
Whose sapless forms he cannot pare –
And if – approaching leafy battlements,

You were to say something colourful to him
Like *Gnomes* or *Toadstools,*
There is no knowing to what lengths his tongue
May run from underneath his hat's straw brim.

Where you stand, beyond his care, days run
Footloose and dangerous with untethered forms;
But where he moves, light is shed on living order
And even darkness does not halt his slow green art –
For then the world is undoubtedly a perfect sphere
Turning easily on branchy axis – and he is no more
Than its attendant moth hovering in a well-kept universe.

Retreat

Time came to find his summer residence gone.
O the furnishings of voluptuous memory –
A car seat and one vessel where hedgerows met
Against a decor of steady blue and shorn gold.
Time came when closed windows winked at him coldly
And through frosty spandrels of greenhouse glass,
Chrysanthemums smugly regarded his retreat
To the cradling depths of the last ditch
To suck his blue finger and sop all heaven
With wrapped remnants of an old tailoring.

Time came, and is not gone, when children
Learned to say *A tramp died in this lane,*
Establishing the presence of a dogged absence,
So that now the memory of him lives a detached life
Like someone drawn by Chagall beyond trees and weather.
Vague repetitions can still summon him to tramp,
Loverless, across directions and a wide sky.

Apple Trees

Once there were voices to answer his own
And affable air was the only prospect
Of the branchy scene to penetrate the house.
The trees merely presented themselves
Whenever he chose to regard them

Until insistent silence turned him
To the tongues of the fire, trivial music
And the farm cat's hungry passing calls;
Although even she wore light leaves for eyes
When she approached him through the trees.

Sometimes one perfect apple found fallen
With rotting fruit occasioned mild surprise,
Softening the bosky gesturing
And sawn branch stumps staring wickedly
From impenitent wooden features.

But he knew the imperceptible advance
Cancelled the road, destroyed the house,
And surrender was inevitable;
The last leaf down to fill his mouth,
The frozen roots to wrap his numb heart.

A Plain Girl

A plain girl moving simply enough
Until love turned her down flat,
Leaving her with her parents' lives to live
And trunk full of embroidered stuff.

She acknowledged her plainness thereafter,
Underlined it rigorously
With all the farm work she could find.
Forgot the knack of easy laughter.

Her sisters watched how her coarseness grew,
Saw time-killing work broaden her hands
And gait, watched her gather a man's strength
To herself in the only way that she knew.

Guardedly her brothers watched her come and go,
Kept an eye on her many distances
As though she were the unpredictable horse
They enclosed in the furthest meadow.

Her meagre words the family understood
And they never forgot to turn away
When, with a quiet ferocity,
She chopped unnecessary piles of wood.

A Childhood

Every evening it is the same.
She stands at the door of the bungalow
And frets the vague dusk with his name
Until he emerges from the shadow
Of colossal trees and tropical flowers,
A diminutive warrior, his pale limbs
Daubed gentian to lessen the powers
Of the company he keeps and claims.
He climbs the verandah reluctantly
Wearing unrelinquished locusts for a whim,
Yet he would curl his sleep near a poisoned tree
Or bring the whole garden to bed with him.

Every evening something goes from her
And calling him becomes a ritual of fear.
Soon there may be no unwilling answer
Or indefinite appearance to draw near.
Moths enter the door, yet he is careless
Of his home and name and seems to stand alone
While she looks into his face, where darkness
Has smeared his lids and marked him for its own.

Ghosts

What you think, is what she mostly is –
The folded look in the garment on the floor,
The photograph moving into place,
Knuckles raining on the widening door.

What you desire, is what she cannot be –
The dream and parlour sorcery are lies.
Only her blood returns on childish feet
With that direct look of hers in other eyes.

What you know, is what you always knew –
His last absence is what you most condone.
He is the black fortune in your cup,
The sensuality you bear alone.

What you fear is what you always feared –
His receding face recedes for ever,
Is passionless and inclined to smile
The friendly smile of a former lover.

A Bereavement

It is a thumping and eternal lie.
It is not two weeks of happiness,
Only blackness with a patina of blue sky.

It is not a rink between promontories
On which to slide triangular sails,
But a smooth launching of random journeys.

Lovely boys, ignore the whispering shell
Whose issue waits to saturate uniforms
Of valour and drown lusts you would propel.

Outstare the audacious winking wave
Whose foaming lace is ephemeral,
Whose blue sheeting palls an impatient grave,

Before promenading sorrow swells again
Filling asylum with postcards unfolding
False seascapes from my shrouded captain

When, like rain, the sea in tiny quantities
Arrives without the wreckage of one bone
Or slimy button for trembling reliquaries.

Gloves

Descending the gloom of early stairs,
I find someone has left
A small complex sculpture in the hall –
Until I see more clearly
It is your gloves lying there,
Fat-fingered, enormous; like gloves
Waiting for a ball-game to commence.

Thinking of your finely cast hands,
I see them quite deliberately
Dropping their tailored impedimenta
Before driving cold morning air.

Yet, settled as bronze,
The gloves' fingers stay curled.
They do not lose their grip.

Coffee

Addiction dampens my brow.
Cups, jugs and percolators contain my life.

When friends ask more than I can give,
I give them coffee.
When my soul craves living waters,
I drink coffee.

Coffee's black depths ingrain my features.
I sit drawn to its dark brewings
Like Beardsley's diabolical women.

I sit sipping and mourning Brazil and Kenya –
Their economy depends on me.
When this consumption is interred with me,
What will the plantation workers do?

Who will manage my estate of cups?

Some to Alice

I am tired of departures.
Footfalls and barely audible words,
When will you cease pattering endless corridors?
Upturned faces flowering dark waters with death,
When will you ultimately submerge?
Trains, air terminals, ships, wooden boxes,
Your confusing efficiency is lethal.
Indestructible matter reduced to dust
Permanently powders these rumpled sleeves –
And heart, soggy as a wet handkerchief,
Will not cease its ridiculous waving.

Alice, child of circumspection,
The gentle tin-can knight departs.
You have managed the whole affair nicely
And politely wave your handkerchief;
But does the nonsensical musical offering,
Indifferently received, recur with surprising overtones?
And would any running jump I made at a brook,
After having turned my back, make me queen?

PLAINSONG
(1981)

Open to the Public

What would they think, those writers, those artists,
If they could return home now to hang
All-seeing windows with their flimsy lengths,
Or shuffle through stiffened rooms with the curious?

Sweet recognitions. Hopeless protestations.
The chair still presiding over unworn carpets of light,
The clock holding one hand across its dead-beat heart;
And the watercolours, drawn from other rooms.

But those instruments, out of tune with time,
Letters unfolded, poems blinded by glass,
Nether garments displayed – and punctual intruders,
Unfamiliar and unloved, haunting every room.

Sunflower

How the sight of that great head
Inflames our endeavours.
And yet, if that head
Possessed one more attribute,
How slowly it would turn away
From our inclinations
Or droop to see
The scientific ladies in pinafores
Recording the true breadth
Of the biggest sunflower in the street
With a linen tape-measure.

And how the mere thought of that head
Can light a dark mind –
Like a flambeau fixed in a corner
Of some chateau, where only this morning
My lord quickly relieved himself
Before pulling on velvet
To face an audience with the sun.

Snapdragons

A fly comes to regard the unwashed dishes
And rubs illusive legs with glee,
While she regards them – and moves
Away to the window framing
The labial velvets of the garden.
She considers the flowers ill-named,
And shrugging off the house,
Augments the warm poutings of afternoon
Thinking she, too, placed in sunny permanence,
Could wear a cat-soft mouth and exhale sweetness,
Could attain that sculptural silence
Apportioned only to flowers and squatting gods –

Until a bee comes to regard rich mouthings
And intrudes with lusty glee –
Leaving her uncertain on the grass
Wondering if she hears beyond
The busy violation of silence,
Glad echoes and amplifications.

Bean-flower

Bunny, can you see today's blue
Precisely occupying the infinite
Green arms of the bean forest
Where the bean-flower hoards nothing
But perfume and that insignia
With which to match coming darkness?

Bunny, when the farmer creases his pillow
And the bean-flower loses its whiteness,
There will be no precise definitions
And no occupation that is not ours.

Elsdon

All day the irises have draped blue velvets
In the window, but now dusk turns blind,
They blacken and stand off with nocturnal trees
As if to say colour is a matter of the mind.

And mind, yielding to the darkness of this place,
Would hang the window with a more pungent flower,
For now I think the gallows creaks the hill,
The castle shrugs off its green pelt, the Peel Tower

Withstands nothing, and the significance
Of three long skulls cannot be re-interred.
Now I know the red dwarf of the hills survives –
Comes spitting meanness in his bloody beard,

Angry as a side-show deformity; comes ready
To pinch my heart blue-black as these
Gathered flowers growing indistinguishable
From the coldness of nocturnal trees.

Elsdon Church

At the cold centre Christ keeps faith,
Faith darkly noosed, faith overshadowed
By rank encircling sycamores
That do not break their rankness
But stand to break God's entrenching stones,
To combat light with gloomy handlings,
To hoodwink with druidical attitudes –

Unless hoodlum wind moves them
To reveal Christ narrowly, piecemeal,
A captive deity, or less;
A lamb caught in a thicket,
A well hewn Jack-in-the-Green –

Where only wilderness rushes down
With constricting light.

Janey's Cottage

It could be said that the lobby
Is the cold centre of the cottage –
Where the new owner has
Temporarily installed a refrigerator.

Or it could be said the lobby
Is where Janey mostly stands
Considering whether to ascend
Or to go through the door for the last time.

It could be thought
Habitual shadows in the kitchen
Are standing there
Preparing some dark cohesion

And that the weak flame
My shoulder-blades see
Climbing illuminated stairs after me,
Is Janey looking for sleep.

Could be, next year, when I have gone,
When builders have admitted the sun
And only a photographer
From *Homes and Gardens*
Would recognise the place as home,

Janey will find unfamiliarity
Hard to wear, will wake
To morning's clucking contentment,
Remember the stream's original course
And braid her vaporous childish hair –

Or, waking to one ringing bell,
Will remember her crabbed front gardening
Hardly stopped at Elsdon Green,
Where God still stands, leaf-lammed,
Cold, but familiar.

Cottage Industry

Eager to rent mountains and a wider sky,
We have rented Janey's Cottage – but
The new owner, eager to sell vacancy,
Has hardly achieved eviction and conversion –

Next year will be different, she predicts affably,
When the cottage will be completely modernised.
Meanwhile, only the bedroom is as it should be –
Frilled with blue nylon, last shadows painted out –

While shadows remain painted in downstairs.
They stand serving time in the kitchen cell,
Fill the thumping sofa and fortified chairs;
Hoard themselves, cold as death, in cupboards.

Next year may be different – more glass, less stone.
Until then, one jammed window nearly lets us see
This awkwardness is personal, is still someone's home –
Allows us a blind of leaves; a complete absence of sky.

Nocturne

Paper music yellows overnight
And remains dedicated to those
Aristocratic effusions dressed in black.
The form is meaningless after all –
Like the names of alien princesses –
And a smell of older remembered instruments
Begins to emanate from the piano.

The nightfall road runs downhill
As though there were a choice,
As though destinations stood still
Beneath allusive measurements of the sky;
And on the far side of town
The dead reach through darkness saying,
Our stones are pushed against the wall.
There is no room. There is nowhere to go.

The Lucky Ones

The lucky ones smile at me.
Their smiles hover like gentle birds
Edging aspidistra forests,
Their extravagant hats float
Against derelict sunsets oiling canvas seas,
And their hands keep very still
Along the arms of rustic seats.

Those who are bareheaded
Are astonishingly young
And their garments begin
To look something like mine.

They pose beyond the borders of deceit –
But, without moving their lips
Or thinnest bones,
They say, quite distinctly,
Come.

Night Sucks Me In

Night sucks me in
With other pale ephemera.
What can I touch now
That is not the colour of darkness
Or the object of your death?

In the lane this morning
The small hen fixed me with her silly eye
While deliberating between early sun
And the receding mildew of shadow
Boxed beyond the barn's half open door.

Balancing her indecision on one fine leg,
Her yellow arabesque was irrefutable,
Her plumage a sleek ardour risen from fire

And beyond her, all the birds sang
Until the dimensions of the valley shattered
And composers who had not recorded birdsong
Since youth, leaned awakened heads
From distant windows to take feverish notes.

All the same, the day's music ends in this.
The least filament of melody
Does not infiltrate night
And I conduct nothing that is not
Silence between intervals.

In the House

In the house the man lies dying.
The woman dies also, but more slowly.
The creaking woman leaves the house
And enters the garden sighing,
Where she leans heavily on the sun's fire
To wrest one flower from the day.
She carries the flower to the man
Saying, *Look, it is open this far.*
And the man regards the powdery star.
Later, the woman leaves the house again
And returns with another flower
Saying, *Now it is open this far.*

The man measures the day's opulence,
Stirs his head, moves his mouth,
Acknowledging a little time
Can make a world of difference.

For Benjamin Britten

The green shutters were back
And the sunflowers looked
To the sea's parallel light
Held taut as a violin string

Until something intervened,
Brushing the sun with black wings.

Now the sea darkens and climbs
Heavily up the untenanted shore.
The lanyards hang slack.
Subdued petals tremble in their suspense –
And we light up the house
Hoping to conjure your voice.

Plainsong
(for Pandora)

I am like that bereaved emperor
Longing for his lovely lady,
But I would not crook a finger
At courteous magicians or
Cry out at shadowy conjurations.

Governing little,
I wear rain on plain sleeves,
Abhor kind fraudulence,
And no longer look for the reality
Of your inattentive face
In the shadows of old photographs
Where you sit in ancient gardens
With an averted gaze, or
At café tables wearing dark glasses.

Love and art never held you fair and square,
And any semblance of your face
Is an uncertainty, a turning away –
And no dark parlour conjuring
Would prove your many departures
Were not of your own choosing.

The Delivery of Fruit

The restaurant shutters are back
And Madame leans out on the morning
Waiting to see the delivery of fruit.
Like the granite figures inhabiting
The rue Armand Henri Rousseau,
She does not move, but her little
Golden heart still moves.
It swings here and there on its fine chain
Locked in a life of its own,
Like the water still swinging here and there
In the bucket someone has left
Standing in the kitchen doorway,
Like the ocean still sidling here and there
On the far side of Madame's granite cliff.

Not that Madame regards unruly waters
Or is moved by her wayward heart.

She is waiting to see the delivery of fruit.

Hôtel des Bains

On the one hand I am all at sea —
On the other, I regard the poplar trees
Pliantly defending the Church of Our Lady.
Boisterous passions and grey lamentation
Have shaped the aspiring granite
That is Our Lady's worn habitation,
But her green guardians, firmly footed in sand,
Possessors of less rigid attitudes,
Keep countless edges clearly defined in wind.
It rained yesterday, it rains today,
But dark leaves turn to make light of weather
And tune my mind to a song of yesterday
Because I think the trees peculiarly French.
I hear *Roses are shining in Picardy* —
And roses appear to be shining on every branch —
Although love is not watching by the poplars
To a plaintive accompaniment.
There is nothing but rain and parked cars.

On the other hand, against the firm line of the sea,
The tallest and prettiest girl in France
Stoops low, like an anxious swan, preparing coffee,
Cherishing each potion as though she were Iseult —
All because she will not wear her spectacles.
I could tell her, if language were not difficult,
If, like the trees, we had common tongues to share,
About the music in my head and inconsequential
Explosion of roses filling the leaden square.
I could tell anyone, if experience had not taught me
Language is safer left furnishing the mind.
But smiling, Mademoiselle approaches with coffee.
We both smile. Our informative smiles are splendid,
As celebratory today as they were yesterday.
Slowly I drink my brew. Slowly I break my bread.

Grasshopper

Like a lost brooch, he keeps
The colours of the grass to himself;
Keeps unwinking and forever, the river,
The valley path, the alpine pass.

There is no leaping from this moment.
The harebell is resolute, and knowledge
No longer spells out its own name
Or rusts green armoured vigilance, for

His symmetry maintains the steady heights,
The horned mountaineers shaking thin bells –
And passing bare legged youth carrying
Nothing but wild fruit in cans.

The cretin's laugh told you what you know.
The nearest station is lost in mist
Under cold scree and towering snow.
The next train never comes.

Hans Andersen in Venice

The nocturnal city matched his dream.
Pure silver and black silences,
It was, like the moon, sheer invention –
A city whose thoroughfares a mermaid could navigate,
An image a mermaid could retain in her glass,

Until morning light revealed the mourning wreck.
The whole thing was on a loose footing
And he had simply stepped
From one treacherous Adriatic vessel to another.

The quick ambassadorial scorpion was the first
To take him by the hand
And rats, wearing nothing but their business suits,
Appeared from choleraic fissures,
But not to see the visiting poet.
Oh, he would have discovered the city's heart,
But not by way of dirty runnels or infernal chasms;
Or he would have loitered in a paved square.
Had one bird bared her throat beguilingly in dry tracery.
But the matronly Venetian bird, inclined to stoutness,
Fouled his step and fixed him with a manic eye,
And only sideways at that,
Until he was nothing but outline
Waiting to contain a wash of darkness –
Unless, all animation, he could catch the new life-line
Slung from dry footed vineyards and steam pell-mell
Back to the certain rigour of a northern dream.

Cambridge

Cambridge daffodils are punctilious,
The weather a handful of mirrors.
Wind, rain, sun and snow glissade
To be first to settle cold barometers.
The near-sighted abandon bookstalls
To mark the floor of the restaurant
While tired-faced women in curls
And glass jewellery complain quietly
Across the tables of their animosity
About the bravura garments of the young.
Appetites quiz the restaurant windows
Then disappear in the weather's furore.
Snow re-threads architectural furbelows
And settles on a passing negro's head
To dissolve from whiteness in striding darkness –

And we divine Pushkin in our coffee cups.

Crowland Abbey

Ah, such heat, such infernal skylines.
How can you bear it?
The tarry road sucks your pilgrim feet.
Crowland's clock is tarry too,
Sticky as a Pontefract cake,
And the roses stand martyred
In their own flamey colours.

Why burn here, swelling
The hatless company of broken saints?
Water of life runs cold from the gardener's tap,
The yew tree's shade is almost dependable
And beyond the door, total immersion
Awaits you in breath-taking gloom,
Where one gala swoop to God
Could be made on tantalising bell ropes.

Why not consider saintliness?
Abbot Theodore's skull,
Emptied by the Danes,
Still sanctifies the abbey
And is white with holiness,
Precious as a collector's blown egg
In its little plain glass box,
Is sweet with death and martyrdom
Like a Mexican funeral meat.

Ah, he would acknowledge heat too,
If he could inhabit his sweetness again –
And fear – seeing all the fields
Of Lincolnshire on fire.
Danes again, he would say.
No, just farmers burning autumn fields,
You would explain.
But other terrestrial fires still burn.

Pastime

*When I play with my cat, who knows if I am not
a pastime to her more than she is to me?*
MONTAIGNE

Madame cat, for distraction,
Has entered my Lord Montaigne's tower
And ascends to his lofty room
Where she finds him, like herself,
Hardly employed and at a loss for words.
She approaches him amorously
Hoping to provoke him to playfulness
And is completely diverted when he
Relinquishes his pen to offer her
The complexity of his form – until a shadow
Promising more substance and movement
Catches her attention, whereupon
She leaves my Lord without ceremony
To paw the room's dark perimeter.

Finding nothing there, she remembers
Nothing is what mostly concerns her –
And settles in a contemplative attitude
Where my Lord can no longer reach her
Without rising from his chair.

Heat

Why am I here?
The whole city smells worse than an old woman,
People uncover their monkey toes,
And waiters ignore me
Just because they can see
I am really somewhere else.

Back home
The curtains are on the currant bushes,
The cows are chewing the shade,
And someone walks down to the fish ponds
With a large umbrella.

Man Dancing with the Moon

She had been grudging
While he drained his glass –
A virgin face frosting his window,
A cold glance in his mirror
Until, turning once more,
She saw him fill soft pumps
With impatient feet
And stand tiptoe on darkness.

Rightly shod, it was easy after all.
Lifting his arms, he partnered brilliance
And stepped with her one, two, three,
Never a foot wrong, in the endless hall
Of scintillating company.

Chair

With a leg at each corner,
Like McGonagall's cow,
Your attitude is perfectly right;
The only possible compromise
Between the perpendicular
And wholly horizontal.

The complexity of your legs,
Expertly upheld,
Will keep a lion at bay.

Given a push, you enable
The whey-faced to smile at flower beds.

Given a coat of gold,
You support sovereignty –
God even – properly positioned.

She Played the Trumpet in My Bed

(for Dr Bowdler)

She played the trumpet in my bed
And never failed to raise my head.
Her low notes in a minor key
Were studies in intimacy
And preludes to that highest note
I urged her on to every night.

And yet, that note I feared the most.
I feared the ornaments were lost,
I feared the stars would be blown out;
I feared my neighbour roundabout
Would lift his own dark handsome head
Divining brass in my low bed.

And that is what my neighbour did.

Bell-Boy

Papageno treads the boards
For the second time round.

He is still recognisable
Although he has put on starched linen.
I know him by his extreme youthfulness,
His devotion to his instrument
And his hopeful air.

He is sure we will all rise again
To clothe undying appetites
On hearing ascending euphony.

Sea

If that vast salt expanse
Should slowly drain away
Or give up its blue body
Entirely to the ardour of the sun,
What dry animals we should become –

Curious at first maybe, picking
At the skeletons of Time's wreckage,
But disconsolate at last
And doomed as dinosaurs
Thirsting at small ponds
Clogged with toy craft –

Before going mad, mad,
On a diet of fresh water.

A Different Kettle of Fish

Hoarded sequins in a gleaming vessel
Somewhere else,
But visible.
Each fish wrought
In pure silver,
Their eyes clearly semi-precious,
Their flesh something to be imagined.

Or stewing in their own juice,
In a logie pan,
Their eyes white with heat,
Their mouths grim with mortification,
The air about them questionable.

But never
The fish of the day,
Just coming to the boil.

The Duke of Wellington

Now the Iron Duke waits for the bus,
There is much bronze in his make-up.
He is very elevated,
Handles his sword with distinction
And allows his cloak to fall
On a few volumes of supportive literature;
But there is no hauteur or patronage in his attitude,
Although he commands advancing traffic
With a pertinacious eye
And lends his name to the big hotel.

It is sedentary townspeople who are
Obliged to turn their backs on him.

Exiles

The banished prince
Loses his charm and waistline
And dies, but slowly,
Drinking his own health.

The adroit European
Forgets his profession,
Invents a new shirt-making machine
And moves among those
Not dissimilar from himself.

Spider

The thread is held.
He swings, he runs, he must,
From twiggy angles
Where flowers happen.

He measures, he scrambles
Before rain's impeding jewels
And waits, waits for
The winged meats to snag

When, without fe-fi-fo-fum,
He will wind and store,
Because he must.

In Front of the House

The streets of childhood are not far away.
They remain quiet and empty mostly, places
Where cries and crying can still be heard.
The rag-man trundles his incoherence,
One of the last beggars drags a foot
And his maniacal singing in the gutter,
And speed is something attained by
The wooden traffic of ingenious boys.
Every day, larger than the house,
The milkman's horse calls to trim the hedge
And deposit dung for superior gardens.

Soon the street photographer will call
With his box of tricks – and if you stand
By the front gate with freshly combed hair,
He will place his black cloth on his head
And sentence you to eternal proprietorship.

Afternoon

The child, like someone in a dream,
Lies awake on the curled red sofa
In the darkening tenement room
Watching the woman let down her hair,
Vaguely astonished to learn age
Possesses such abundance to groom.

Knowing long hair is something worn
Only by children and illustrated queens,
She sees in the overmantel's reflection
Someone other than the grimy-handed woman
Plaiting hair in unfathomable water,
Where swan vases swim palely on and on.

Daisies

In the closed ranks of tall daisies
Igniting the far corner of the garden,
An exultant child lies hidden.
If he moves, the abrasive forest
Scrapes his limbs; if he breathes,
The rank odour annihilates;
And all the while he anticipates
The obscene scrambling of spiders.

Soon he must leave the forest's stinking floor –
But now, through the branchy imposition,
He sees an endless azure vision
Hung with golden pennants – and knows
A voice from the house will never find him.

Boy in a Mask

The skin fits.
The ferocious smile
Fixed, haunts
Store and pavement.

Anonymity has gone to his head.
He is a warm god
Moving in a temple forecourt
Ruling surprise.

Surprise possesses him.
He is so different.
His features pour
Into moulded darkness.

His garments clothe
Endless attitudes.
His eyes flash
Narrowed truth.

Pen and Ink

Concerning my ancestors – they were
Mostly people of culture and philanthropy.
Take great-grandfather for instance.
In the street where he lived, he was
The only man who possessed a pen and ink –
And all the neighbours, at one time or another,
Borrowed both.

And he was truly philanthropic.
When the O'Shaughnessys proved to be
A family of endless affairs,
He would send the pen and ink to them, saying,
Tell them to keep the pen and ink
and I'll borrow them when I need them.

Starlight

Three kings embark on a long journey
Under the dry acres of the moon,
Whose light is well disposed,
But of no special significance.

It is the nailhead light
Of one sparky planet
That draws them on –
Although at times,
One king thinks the star
Has the look of crayon
Drawn on dark paper;
While another thinks it
Looks no more than a sliver

Of silver pasted on indigo;
And the third king, observing
A certain unsteadiness,
Thinks the heavenly guide
Trembles on its cotton thread.

Boatman

He will be there soon
If, like some monarch,
He can look evenly
Into successive mirrors

Until the tunnel's rocks
Are obtrusive cattle,
Draped velvets,
Anchored at the edge of light

Where, red as his coat,
A roof slants away
From trees and water,
Housing dry satisfactions.

Miss Grant

Oneself Miss Grant,
Sufficient in the white walls
Around the necessary furniture
And one dog to talk to by the fire.

Resigned to the baker's call,
The plopped frog on the parlour floor
For excitement, framed relations
And receded nephews in naval attire.

One Bessie cow to pursue
In the deep drenched garden endless
To the dripping honeysuckle
And boulders on the lip of the loch.

No distraction or running water,
But the mountainous moving picture,
The pouring stream and tile-hung
Curtain of rain before the sun's lick.

One life to finish
According to the windowsill's book
In Gaelic, as big as a tombstone
And appropriately black.

An East Wind

My lady looks across the frozen lake
And regards the future of her desolation.
Who now will keep snowy walks
Or bring expiring plumes of punctual horses
To the elevation of her door?
Love will not keep pin-toed swans
Awkwardly questioning the nature of ice
And knowing this, my lady regards
The stature of the kylins
Keeping the furthest rim of the lake
And is no longer sure of their expression.
Where once she saw twin guardian laughter,
She now thinks she sees
Petrification of an immanent roar
And wrings the cold jewels and bones of her hands.

Aloof from snuffling canine ancestry,
The kylins stare across the lake
In stony resolution at weather and departures.
Now the leonine features predominate
And the heavy paws pin down their spheres
While they regard my lady's dwindling estate.
And they do nothing more than this,
Or care what mad songs she hums to winter's instruments,
Or what history she mouths to infirm reflections
Caught in frosty spandrels of high windows.

Torturer

I thought you were nothing
More than a dry stain that is
Found on the page of a book
Where once an insect,
Having reached a certain line,
Was crushed to death
By the reader.

But histories never
Properly confined you.
Daily you make your mark
On wide news-sheets.
Your hood is off,
You display your teeth.
Like the shirt on your back,
They are in good repair.

Barbarians

They shook the south gate of our city
Threatening destruction.
Their strength was remarkable,
Their footwork and aerobatics even more so.
Yet, when we had contended long enough,
We found we were still many
And that flowers grew where there had been none.

They enter the north gate of our city
Threatening reconstruction.
Their strength, too, is remarkable.
They can wield a ball and chain
And rattle their pockets at the same time.
When we have contended long enough,
It will be too late.

It Will Never Stop

It will never stop snowing now,
But no one seems to know this.
It has all been seen before
And is to be expected they say.
So much delicate application
Inevitably alters familiar features.

Now the junk yards resemble holy mountains,
They forget the colour of corrosion.

Worse still, they believe
There is always room in the sky.

Garden Sphinx

She remains a work of art
And will not flay you
With unanswerable questions.
She will not crack her lips apart
And destroy the serene pose;
But waits until you come by night
To question her heredity,
The intention of rounded paws
And ambiguity of face,
Divine, yet almost pretty,
As though some moonlit intervention
Had quietly taken place
By Boucher or Fragonard.
Interrogate the kindness
Of her sculptured breasts,
And you will come to regard
Her as something silence bred
Against standing trees.

Turn your back on the great house,
Touch the damp monumental head
With your glove of moonlight
And she will tell you two things –

How cold hewn stone grows in darkness.
How heavily it leans on earth at night.

Centaur

Not that we do not believe in
The immobility of your furious charge
Across our line of vision –
And do not think we imagine
All the actions of your ancestors
Were more beautiful than our own.

Your behaviour has been
Far from exemplary,
And now one related to you
Stands in the municipal park
With exposed armature
Staining a classical leg.

But if you were to advance further,
Crack your jaw and say,
The horse and rider are one,
We might stamp our hindquarters
And throw back our heads in agreement.

A Sensation

It can happen just like that.
You look through a carriage window and see
A rusty trellis of wild convolvulus
Screening the backs of gritty tenements,
The frail trumpets mouthing white tranquillity.

Or you will see leafless apple trees
In the gardens of suburban bungalows
Splashing fruit against uninterrupted blue,
The colours a sudden exaggeration like those
On canvas awaiting Russian dancers.

Or you will turn a sunny corner where
Black people dressed in colours anyhow
Pose a wedding against a wooden church,
And you will feel happiness is a rocket
Ignited there and exploding now.

Or someone will turn a dusky corner
From allotments, his quiet hands and wrists
Powdered with earth, his bicycle ridden
With flowers – and later you may recall
Flower carts drawn by Japanese artists.

Young Man in a Railway Carriage

You sleep easily on the train
Wearing hat, sweater, gloves and socks –
All of them knitted in jubilant colours –
Reminding me love once took
Winter's children, goose-greased them
And stitched them in.

You are certainly stitched in.
I watch the pattern of beasts
Breathing evenly on your chest,
But think what a well dressed
Slender young man you would be
Without this love –

How, like me, you would journey
Terribly awake, sweetened by fumes
From the Gothic biscuit factory
And oppressed by evening's emptiness
Piling up on the thinning horizon.

Cooling Towers

It is as though some surrealist artist,
Having been at work, has successfully made
His footling point of disproportion – yet
Somehow people live in such a landscape
Waking belittled, every morning,
Under a roof of smoke to a solid sky
That never moves from one side of the house.

Something more than familiarity and the cost of living
Keeps them beneath so much oppressive usefulness,
Something more than distant prospects
Of slender chimneys camouflaged with earth colours
And sky-blue paint – trompe-l'œil that fools no one.
So they remain where nothing can be painted out,
Quietly fuelling their fearful-looking giants –
Whose name can evoke an image of rain-wet turrets
Standing aloof in suburban laurels.

One Neighbour

The evening puts on its lurid garments,
The tractor puts on a little more rust,
And both sink without recrimination
In the waiting silence of the west.

Mary, put on your evening pinafore,
For you must quietly do the same.
There is no one to haul the lobster pots,
There are no cattle to call back home.

The Cuillins are in a towering rage,
Further off than childhood stands Portree,
And a weird light crowns barbaric Rhum
Where one more day dies ritually.

But Mary, hug your faith that says
Cats live on air and the warted cow
Meets no pain by the livid loch whose road
Brings Christ and His priest to you now –

For your one neighbour still gives one light
And has scythed through your grass accurately,
A straight path you can tread tomorrow,
Like a prophet walking a divided sea.

Wild Musk

Wild musk flowers still fill a bucket of water by the door,
A gift from her one neighbour she intends planting;
But she does nothing more than come to stand there regarding,
Without rancour or delight, the feverish effusion.

Musk is from far off, like mainland flowers sold from wide windows;
And far off is the forbidden nearby burn and cramping hill
Visitors climb sometimes to see mountains that are always there.
All, all is far off outside the sinking croft; although once
She trudged the devious road to serve the island's great house.

She lifts her head, regards her one neighbour's croft
And shields her eyes. Yes, he has scythed a dry path down
To her door through high grass and will soon appear to exercise
The new heifer on a rope, when she could watch the frantic frieze –
As once she watched dancers elaborating vases in the great house –
And *then* she could plant the musk.

But she has other things still to do, and turning inwards,
She fills a bowl with water, comes to the door again
And washes her hair in evening light.

The Pleasure of Ruins

This is the picture you took of me on Skye.
It is a very funny photograph –
To look at. I remember how your cry
Startled me at the time, causing me to turn
Quickly as though I were loaded with crime.
I am so distorted, half thin, half fat,
Like a comedian who is told to mime
A look of foolish surprise worth remembering.

I remember something else startled me too,
Just before you called my name. Something
That was once a rabbit humped into view
In the long grass of the ruined churchyard
And the obscenity of its enormous head
And suffering was, momentarily,
The only reality I understood,
Obscuring your presence and the bald mountain.

Even now, it is the soft blinded animal
And wordless agony filling the dereliction
Of a holy place that I recall,
Against a background vague with mountains
And transitory love – and I am sure,
If you remember at all, you see less than this;
Although I do not know where you stand any more
Or if I am anywhere in the picture.

Going

Yes, I am quite the artist. I can still
Draw the snow filled park from memory –
The trees, the lake, the frozen statuary.
But I'm second rate. I have no skill
Capturing the human face – not even yours,
Animated or grave, posed against blank skies
And traditional romantic properties.
But this is not surprising of course,
For I was uncertain of your expression –
And in the city's invading mist, the snow
Was preparing to run away – and I know
The lake was losing its firm resolution.
And you – you were merely part of the scene
Surviving the advances of the season –
One of the effects going, going, almost gone.
But at no affordable bidding of mine.

FORTY POEMS

Invitations to Voyage
with Mr Alfred Wallis, Artist Extraordinary

1

Quickly, put on another coat
And we shall advance on Labrador
In a banana-coloured boat

Masted each end, funnelled twice,
Carrying smoke blown forward,
Soft as hair and blue as ice,

On an uphill sea sweetly white,
As the all over sky would be,
If the sky were all over white

And not grass-green with bergs tossed high –
Like hay-cocks in the field back home
Where the harbour lane hits the sky.

2

A bad business
Surviving this dirty momentum.
There's no room for running a ship
Between dish-water and a fallen sky.

The rocks are almost done for.
Their everlasting blackness,
Like our pitchy vessel,
Is grinding down.

Hereabouts we coast more rocks
Footing a streak of mean green,
For hereabouts colour ran out.
It's useless looking for a sunny arm at danger point –

And directly overhead,
Those barely discernable points
Are not lustreless stars.
They are washed over nail-heads
Holding up the weather.

Think of yourself –
Not heavy coals and bad news.
The cargo can sink or swim.

3

A tidy sort of a day, too bright for drama,
So he will make an unusually short trip
Taking in the town's architecture
Of house-fronts, warm as drying sails, lining
Sand-coloured streets against a sea-blue sky;
And he will avoid the harbour's certainties –
A saucerful of briny, a lopsided vessel and
One lighthouse, white as a blind man's stick –

Then return to Back Road West, where he will
Fill the kettle and contemplate a last voyage;
There is board enough and ship's black paint for that.
But he's in no hurry, and if Mr Nicholson brings
Mr Wood or anyone else to darken his open door
With curiosity, well, he may nod, he may smile –
Although they take his light – but he will keep
His ground and the kettle on the boil for himself.

Cerne Abbas

Herculean, all sex and violence,
The white giant still keeps the hill.
Recumbent in the grass – running
Sideways too, like a dreaming animal,
Advancing full frontal nudity
And making a really firm stand
With a wave of his airy club,
He fixes everything with four eyes.

Never sleeps or descends light;
Descends only in darkness
To flat foot it abroad
Without fee, fi, fo or fum,
Staring dumbly through low windows,
Moony faced, begging maintenance
From white-fingered dreamers.

Cottage Orné

His castle is his home – but his dream
Stands by the sea facing the approbation
Of the bay and tumultuous applause.
Even so, far from home, he is not sure
Those long green arms keep navigable order
And mistrusts head-on salty winds
That grime quizzed and quizzing windows.

So mostly, far from home, he retires
From retirement and ordination of the day
To the lordship of one room whose
Rear window frames a measured vista
And telescope angled for heavenly night –

When he can swing that enlarging eye
To scan ownership of a brilliant order
He could still learn to emulate –
If he did not fear the blinding intervention
Of mothy wings – or a sudden view
Of baby and cook raising fat fists.

Ship in a Bottle

The Doldrums a hardened gaiety;
Green and blue resolutions
Undrinkable as salt water.

The craft drily rigged to
Employ a zealous wind now
Sleeping in a silted cavern.

The crew below deck refusing
What is everlastingly ahoy –
That dark sun afore,
Funnelled somehow. A stuck plug.

It is true; the sea stays put.
Destinations never drain in.
To port and starboard,
Beyond glassy air,
An indistinct world heaps,
Out of all proportion,
Foreign fabrications
Without runnels or moisture –
From whose harbourless geography
A large eye sometimes drifts
And bears down in a
Starless cloud of shadow
Like a suddenly attentive god
Ascertaining fixed order –
Before moving off to remoteness.

Hare in the Moon

He is no longer here.
It is the wind trembling
Heartlessly in the corn.
He has taken a fearful leap
To god-head in the moon
Where he is darkly heaped up –

For men rarely go to the moon
Leaving the world turning on,
Turning slowly to verdigris –
The black grass bent to silver –
And when they do, they go ill-dressed,
They go monstrously shod,
Too encumbered to leap,
Too properly puffed to run.

How a heaped-up god could laugh at this.

Song of the Motorcyclist

On the road to Scotland
I saw her combing out her hair.
In Northumberland, beyond the river,
On the road to Scotland
I saw her combing out her hair.

As I flew by her window
I looked down to see
Light descending a bank
To enter her room and hold her there –
Pouring out her northern hair –

Hold her there until I close my eyes.

Solitaire

Moonlight restored the window,
Threw down a window on the floor.
'On this floor I could dance,' she said
And lifted a rose to her loosened hair,
Lifted her arms to the partnering air.

Waltzing in corners of darkness,
Darkness embraced her briefly there.
Turning in orgies of solitude,
A single perfume veiled her hair.
'On this floor I can dance,' she said.

The Indifferent Horseman

I see the youthful Coleridge here and now
Rising, come Sunday, to the reality of bad grace.

No, he won't carry a bucket to the car,
But influenced or not, he may drive his dingy can
To the nearest car-wash to be ingeniously rained upon,
To be miraculously and most colourfully mopped –

Maintaining still, a horse should wash and brush itself down.

Aquarius

Where is Aquarius the water-carrier?
Can't he see Earth has the face of an old woman
And a garden of nothing but paper flowers?

Where is he with his two fine pitchers?
The stand-pipes are empty, fire is running down
The railway cutting and our children are at home.

The sky is heartlessly blue, but not empty.
It is still all-accommodating; but he's hanging about
Waiting too long for darkness and showy definition.

At Home

Supporting their trees,
The islands of shadow
Can be seen from the house.
He sees them, plans quietly
And leaves the house
By the french window.

Catching the mood of
The twelve o'clock sun,
He travels lightly across
The lawn carrying nothing
More than wine and a book

Until he arrives at
The border of shade
And slings himself up
To leafy accommodation,
From where he hopes to see

The girl next door
Compromised with the sun,
From where he hopes not to
Hear an alien voice calling
His name from the house.

Hearing only an insect drone,
He regards the hot sky
And letting fall his reading matter,
Gives thought to suspended lives –

Before drinking to them all.

The Radio

What once she had been –
A presence in the house.
What once she had been –
A voice in the room,
A voice in the next room
Talking, talking;
Conversational and subduing,
Making one the dramatic intent
Of other voices, other instruments.

What once she had been –
His sole informant,
Half heard, understood;
A reason for occasional music
Loosely composed,
Performed on distant piers.

A reason for rising,
Obliquely tuning himself to
Another day's dismissed silence.

While the Sun Shines

'Mother should be in the picture,' someone said.
The camera lowered and he ran into the house,
For where else should he find her?
'Come and have your picture taken,' he called
To where she fought a softened room overhead.
'Now, just as I am?' she asked, lowering her guard.
'Yes, right now,' he answered impatiently,
'Just as you are – and while the sun shines.'
Turning to the mirror, seeing herself as she was,
Swiftly she disowned her apron, curbed her hair
And altered her mouth to what it no longer was.

Entering the garden, a willing but pressed personage,
She said 'You must take me as I am.'
'Oh we will – we always do,' they laughed.
'Stand there by – but not obscuring the roses.'

And she stood there, enduring company,
Just as she was – smiling, smiling, smiling.

A Formal Goodnight
Hardyesque

Full moonlight fell everywhere
Altering the city's garden air
Where two stood saying good-night.
'Oh Lord, let this loving be right.'
She said to no god in particular.

Pale inseparable ghosts they were;
Oh, he could not have enough of her –
Until one last concluding kiss.
'How I hate leaving you like this.'
He said for no reason in particular,

Other than the lateness of the hour;
For he could discern time beyond her
By angling his wrist at the moon –
And his last train would be leaving soon
For one destination in particular.

Aware of his arm's furtive movement,
She stared long with sad contempt
Divining his silvered mask and knew,
In her bleaching bones, they were through
   – with nothing in particular.

Ferns

The ferns in the lean-to conservatory dissolved light,
Made you feel you were pushing around under water
Or still wearing your green summer eye-shade.
They drifted on whitened shelving from pots
Decorated with ruched crêpe papers – and one fern
Stood in a fluted container someone had fashioned
From an old gramophone record of black shellac.

They clouded out the glazed slope of sooty sky,
Curtained the dining-room window with filmy green
So that in the house too, you wavered in a marine wash,
Spoke slow-mouthed to the woman with fronded hands
Or woke, like Yadwigha, on the chaise-longue of red plush
Still dreaming the jungle hung silently at your back –
Until someone put on the light and moved about.

Privet

There, the trees grow wild,
Are not shaped by hedged minds,
But incline seaward with extended arms,
Incline homeward in uncut garments,
Green, white – the colours of rain.
Are pure impulse, airy angels,
Yet womanly in their provocations
And tall perfumed airs.

And once windows are opened
On their summery surveillance,
We say we cannot return to town –
And keep doors open to
Languorous cloudings,
Breathy insinuations.

Copycat
(Happisburgh)

I could live here –
Keep a cat framed in the front window.
Keep the sun waiting on the front doorstep.
Visitors to the church could leave their cars
Under the sway of my tree, pause to appraise
The simple purity of my snowberry bushes
And the possibility of a similar tenancy.

At night I would
Wait for moths and angels to lose their footing.
I would look into the fixed eyes of my cat
And gravely he would look back at mine.
Together we would listen to the dead singing
Their faintly sad song at the foot of the cliff
And be thoughtfully entertained.

104

Happisburgh

Water of true life still overflows the stone cup
Standing unbroken in God's stone house on the hill
And every ever encircling angel is musical.
Seeing is hearing the music of zither and harp

For time smashed the brilliantly blinded windows
Only to reveal salvation in unremitting light.
Listen – the music is eternal and our birthright
And we drown in measured darkness we cannot oppose

While working waters of the world erode the hill
Moving with consummate passion this way and that
To orchestrated music we can only wonder at,
Music trillion-stringed and seemingly eternal –

Waters only fair as the seemingly fair day
And black as the anguished confusion of night,
Refusing to return our engulfed dead to the light
For commemoration where the green hill falls away.

Yet where it falls away, the cliff-top corn still flows
And the lighthouse wading the bread-coloured field,
Gay as a barber's pole, hard as sweet rock unfurled,
Is charged with certain power that nightly comes and goes.

St Christopher

It is true, some things never change.
Always there are bridges to be crossed
When bridges are down and rivers are up,
Furiously dark with opposition –
And love held high can prove a burden.

Love, childish love, fording frequented water,
Long-haired Faith's small flying angel –
You will be set down soon on the furthest bank
Where death is distanced to another hill
Or road running hard in the opposite direction;
Where the horizon mills grind out their bread
And the bookish man believes he can still
Stand apart to hoist his meagre lantern.

Swincombe

Wild boar lived in the valley until men came.
Men lived in the valley until Black Death came.

There is pity in the order of things.

The wild boar left nothing but half a name –
And men left a little church with a cracked bell.

Flying Angel

The Earth Angel leaves his house.
The moment the door closes behind him
He lifts to a good height, quickly
Gaining confidence and the garden gate.
In the house there was talk above his head
Of spring – and yes, in the long lane
Where the world will witness
Heavenly aviation and outriding birds
Drop two-note asides, he sees clearly
A new whiteness has fallen everywhere.

From a passing car, a glassy face
Smiles affirmation, and he bears
Down the hill in silent exultation

Until someone steps into the lane
And he is forced to hover endlessly.
Impatiently the Earth Angel looks
Down his nose at conversational lowliness
And, sighing, turns his eyes heavenwards.
Heaven is sublimely blue, but empty –
And from vacancy, vertigo's swift
Visitation causes him to give thanks
For being firmly held in the arms
Outstretched of an earthly father.

The Joker

One Christmas the parlour door
Opened very slowly of its own accord
 And a bloodied head peered in
The festooned room without speaking a word.

The fun froze in our mouths –
Until slowly the grisly head smiled at us.
 No, it was not someone's head,
It was only my uncle's wicked taunting face

All covered with lipstick.
Still anchored to the opened parlour door,
 He half entered the room
Revealing the wonderful gift he bore –

A giant box of chocolates –
A great golden nugget ribboned with red.
 The bloody mask smiled again.
'I'm taking these to Clara's place,' it said.

Santa Claus

He's here again without having changed his coat,
And driving hard still his twiggy-headed team
As though his destination were elsewhere.
He's well this side of windless darkness now.
The forest's dwindled to one powdered tree
And the fixed attention of resurrected robin.

Saint, tree and bird are stiff with formality,
But they are no more cold than the snow is cold –
This purely sweet untrodden sheen – on which
Ten airy beings have set down greeting words
In linked lettering of apparent gold.

108

Winter

Lord, now the world is cold
And Lord, now the world is hard.
The hills are white with worry,
The hair of the fields too, is white,
And the dry dove turns slowly
On the garden's frozen ornament.
Lord, the road to your house runs black,
The ditch ferns bend under their glass
And clearly, holiness is frozen in the water stoup.

Lord, now our barns are greater
And in their taut dimensions
Any new-come child would be lost.

Lord, now the world grows colder.
You must feel it hardening still
Like lead shot in the palm of your hand.

All Hallows Eve

Is it true the barriers are down tonight?
It is true there is a feeling of something
Giving way and thinly falling.
Perhaps it is merely a matter of leaves.
Or birds even.
A robin falls repeatedly from fine music
To gorge last grapes in flaming dishevelment,
Shites my yard with purple dye
And rising, sings again, something about
It being good to feast before darkness.

Even if it is only a matter of leaves, tonight
I'll not step outside light's conjured circle,
Shuffle darkness on a hardening ground.
And push narrowing blood through palings
That were once luxuriant –
To meet the form of determined coldness
Risen – from heaven knows where.

Snow

In books the snow keeps falling,
Or has already set the scene – snow
Whiter than the pages on which it falls.

When men were asleep snow came flying, you read.
That year elk and stags froze to death in the forest.
Cold in the earth and the snow piled above thee!

Pausing, you consider the brittle blue
Of the book-shaped window – until it darkens
Against the thick dusk of ephemeral snow.

Blindly, you turn to your window-shaped book.
In one more wintry chapter people are suffering
And singing still in the amazing unaltered air.

Revenants

Thinnest interventions – we could return then,
Not heavy with tragical will and usurpation
Like Ligea – and not home to endure hauntings –
But we could walk again through old French towns
Composed to stand for ever, to be as once we were,
A party to loose swallows, alien and perfectly at home.

Yes, we could return to construe the endless ways
Of cut stone and uncut flowers running on and on –
Yet remain, like outside shadows on church steps,
Weightless and of no consequence still
To black-bloused women employed in rivers,
Or gardeners ordering the vigilance of
Denim scarers in fruit trees above lily clumps.

And if Madonnas in walls let down sweet admonitions,
We could acknowledge such high seriousness – but
Decline their heaven for not being a dwelling
Of countless rose and viny gardens all joined.

Brittany Scarecrows

They are up in the trees again
In their sky-blue suits and sunny hats
Filling unairy spaces between branches
All ready to turn up straw features
From straw brims to sight appetite
And shake out furiously explosive arms.

Their maker should be in the house
Scouring pans and cleaning jars
With one eye on the window
Ready to assist his henchmen.

But he is down by the green canal
With a rod thinking 'cherries are ripe'.

Normandy Head-dress

She is under a cloud.
The cloud rests lightly
On her formal head
Whitely, without weeping.
It has been finely wrought up,
Vapourish, but is now
Beautifully settled
As piled snow.

Somewhere in the blue
There is another cloud
Drifting freely,
But not aimless.
It will descend soon,
Entirely enamoured,
Float to her side all knowing,
Ascend with her to heaven –
Not without purpose.

Almondtears

Woke early in Armentières
This side of the dirty summer Alps.
Saw no one at the railway station,
Saw no one in the sleeping streets,
Save you, mademoiselle, save you –
And soldiers, soldiers, still singing
The song of your dead cold mouth.

No Play

No play today.
Empty stadia.
Melancholy kingdoms, damp domains.
Farms foundering in their sties.

Rain, rain, subduing lusty kennels,
Armouring forests against sullen marksmen
Where deer outlive the cold day
Under heavy awnings.

Mirrors, brocades slowly tarnishing.
And a king enclosed somewhere
Banging on veiled windows.

Boring. Boring.

How far the rain has come
Without changing garments.

Fire

A whiff of sulphur,
A smell of fast burning
As when a match is struck,
Or I file my nails.

A smell of burning,
Of skin blistering
Under scorching flame,
As when a painter strips a door.

A smell of burning
Not redolent of exhausted flowers,
Straw and viny leaves, sweet
Survivals of yet another year.

An unwanted smell
Of unwanted bones and fat
Beginning to burn
Too near human habitation.

This fire beginning somewhere,
This smell climbing its black column
And assailing me when
I lift my head as if to listen.

Nose

Nose, now we are constrained.
We are held narrowly by
A firm forefinger and fat thumb.
Soon, we shall cease to breathe.

Once I could win by you
Every wild race of childhood,
But now, even the grass of the fields
Can bring us both to tears.

Restraint is fitting and for you
I should not have shirked the surgeon;
But how modesty in a regular nose
Smells of failure.

We should have sprawled together,
Gone to ridiculous lengths,
Shut ourselves in our blind room
Against laughter and emerged

Late, with style – you in the lead.

The Small Dark Hours

The moment you open your eyes
You know they have come again –
Black, bug-eyed, wide-mouthed –
To resume eating your life.

'Do what you want,' you think.
And they do just that –
Until you switch on the light –
When, instantly, they seem

To disappear; but you know
They have resorted to camouflage
In closed cupboards and drawers –
And are waiting

Reflection

Only when you are combing your hair
Or putting on clothes do you appear
Solid enough, properly occupied,
Purposeful even and clear eyed.

But when we come face to neon-lit face
In some mirror-hung public place,
Your eyes, your pestilential skin,
Tell me you are truly beaten.

Or glimpsed suddenly in a shop window,
I confront a face I do not know
At first – black mouthed, all Greek tragedy –
Until surprised into uncertainty –

Uncertain as you always are at night,
When thinly you ghost the black light
Held steady in every window frame –
Too thinly faltering to remain the same.

The Whole Thing

The whole thing could be run backwards like a film.
Waking from a knowledge of total darkness, we could
Cry in a bed on conclusive pain that is all our own
And very slowly, we could unwind from every awfulness
To contract convalescence with sunny scythed flowers
And know that yes, today we will really get in our stride
Before assaulting the green hill up to childhood –
On which chancy summit the whole thing could come
To an abrupt end, like a Truffaut film, with us
Staring wide-eyed, smooth-cheeked – at nothing.

Star

When you turned away from heavy traffic,
A star reached out and touched you.
Didn't you feel the breathless descent,
The astonishing condescension?
Already her influence pales your forehead,
Distinguishing you from all others
As you negotiate the sooty footbridge.

And don't you see, in the dark waste ground,
Something standing there, aching with light?
It is wild hemlock, open still to heaven,
Sustaining constellations – not low ghostliness,
Featureless with futile reproof.

Even the Flowers

Even the flowers hate you.
Loose-tongued, their censure
Breaks every window.
Indoors, you turn to the mirror
For assurance; but silently
They re-arrange themselves
Behind your back.

You open your very own hands
And stare down into them.
Happiness must lie somewhere.
How broken your life-line is.
Unhappiness loosens and falls,
Flooding the fanning valleys.

No matter.
Already you have forgotten
Their simple significant names.

You are

You are almost tragic.
Caught in half-light by
The salt river flowing
Endlessly from its ritual vase,

You could lean forward like
A beautifully anguished tree
Reflecting on truth, but your
Inclination would be misconstrued.

The letters you still hold
Are all written on blue paper,
But you no longer untie them.
What you know, you know by heart.

There is nowhere to go. Beyond
You darkness smooths its steep sides
And this side of the river –
Harsh light insists on nothing.

Regret

Fluent, companionable,
The river ran by my side
With clear intent,
Darkening only when it
Slipped under the bridge.

I thought constancy
Never changed,
But only the low bed
Remains unaltered.

I should have told you
I loved you.

When I think

(Mrs Arbuthnot: see Stevie Smith)

When I think of Mrs Arbuthnot,
I think of you living by the sea,
Living where once you wanted to be;
But I do not see you rising
Or raging wildly with the sea.
Rather, I see you shutting your door
Against the wind's fast embrace
And returning to a curtained view
Of everything in front of you;
Your hair white now, every wave in place –

Yes, when I think of Mrs Arbuthnot,
I think of you, when I do not think of me.

UNCOLLECTED POEMS

Aconites

Winter holds fast,
But a little warmth escapes like sand
Through the closed fingers.
The error is annual and certain,
Letting the pygmy flowers
Make their prompt appearance
Under creaking trees.
They stand with serious faces, green ruffed,
As prim as Tudor portraits.

In the west
The greys and gleam slide in the wind
And only the descended blackbird
Augments the intrepid yellow.

[late 1950s]

Bridesmaids

We were the bridesmaids of war.
We stand fading in borrowed dresses
Frailly armed, supporting cold flowers,
Our heads cloudy with rationed tulle,
Pale impossible copies of the bride.

Meek corps de ballet toeing the line,
We smile, almost happily, knowing
That in the direction of the camera
Nothing waits but future's fat peace
Married to fat grooms, knowing

We can never catch up with the bride,
Play an identical leading role –
Never sail off in a parachute-silk gown
On the arm of a sufficient uniform –
On the arm of a hero badly dressed.

[late 1950s]

Acquaintance

Familiar with the outline
Of your altered shape and battered hands,
They express astonishment when you
Direct a small adventure
Beyond the usual orbit,
Unwisely placing themselves
Between inflexible boundaries
Of measured childhood and your old age.

Yet I have known the lovely face
Posed by sepia aspidistras
Evolve from your traditional smile
And the girl with the hoop bowl out
From the sudden prospect in your eyes.

[1962-66]

Adam and Eve

Pale and awkward, they stand in the vast
Panorama of their restricted loneliness,
Lost in original visions of paradise.
Emaciated, or corpulent, they accompany
Their weighty tree with solemnity
Bedevilled by the coiling serpent
Preparing to steal the luscious scene.

Always they are understandably human, down to
The dimple of their navels, as if they
Came from the giant umbilical cord of God;
And simple Adam bears no deliberate scar
Commemorating Eve's miraculous appearance.

Yet truth hides somewhere in the unbelievable
Narrative of broad leaves and benign beasts,
Like strange faces concealed in puzzle pictures;
And although it would take more than a bit
Of the old Adam to account for everything,
Two figures, quiet as simple reflections,
Move intermittently through a landscape
That is entirely interior; a landscape burning
With the canna and drawn sword simultaneously.

[1962-66]

Aged Ninety-Six

The starched and ministering angels
Resurrect Margaret each morning,
Tearing her from sleep, as though sleep
Were some ultimate unkindness;
When she would cling, blind as a limpet,
To the steep wall between herself
And the dark wash of unfathomable sea.

124

But clinical prising proves her small
And sleep is vanquished like a wayward spirit
Faced with lively crackers and gongs
When they beat her thin ears
With her very own name.

Deftly they assemble the handful of bones,
The sharp remnants of a long life,
Powder and prop them up;
And cry in a loud voice reserved for the deaf
'Now you are beautiful Margaret,'
Leaving her to find the beginning
Of a rapid journey from sanitary love.

[1962-66]

An Approach

Look out Miss Elizabeth Barrett
Here comes an uncommon gentleman
With a conversant tongue who can rhyme
Impetuosity with more words than you would choose.
Furthermore, he knows a world of difference
Between wine and porter.

So look out Miss Barrett,
Look out of your window and brush up your Greek.

[1962-66]

Another Man's Soul Is a Dark Forest
(Turgenev)

Another man's soul is a dark forest you said
And for some time following words strayed
Without meaning the closed paths of my head,
While I remembered the first woods I knew
Climbing the fence with that impenetrable view.

And another man's soul became Hop-o-my-Thumb,
The Little Mermaid and the screaming soldier
Lost in darkness by which they are overcome.
But the tangled despair was all my own.
What you meant is the way woods stand alone,

A little apart, screening the inviolate;
The way six dark firs drawn by Chagall
Stand beyond the stables and enviable state
Of the poet reclining, his head on his coat,
His shirt tail out and his eyes remote.

This malevolent May from where I stood
I saw black cloud boiling like Jehovah's wrath
Above the tentative green of the municipal wood.
Without entering, one bird skirted in the darkness
On two white wings, and snow arrived like madness.

[1962-66]

Arachne

The vain spinner was only vain,
Knowing what perfection she could
Put her hand to. But then again,
It was the not knowing that we
Are no less than gods when it comes
To petty rage and jealousy.
The girl miscalculated there.

So now, featureless and shrunken
She mutely fills the present air
Between the railing and the rose
With her finest work, and wins my
Sympathy. After all, who knows
How often golden gods descend
To reward the sure but humble?

I suspect they rarely unbend.

[1962-66]

Bad Dreams

I still have bad dreams, although
I think the worst dreams have me.
Stairs and lifts take me to awful heights
Where I hang like Harold Lloyd, or fall.
Faceless German soldiers, trailing me
From childhood, close in and bayonet me
To a death in sweating wakefulness.
I stifle in tiny Anderson shelters,
Or pick my way through the dead laid out
In familiar Shaftesbury Avenue.
Sometimes red meat confronts me bloodily.
(This one could be disgorged,
But occasional guilt is easier to bear.)

Good dreams diminish and I forget
To astonish with my abilities
To fly, or dance better than Fonteyn.
Sensual encounters grow rare
And fragments from coloured dreams
Submerge like lost tesserae.

Sometimes I recognise my terror
For the dream it is and haul myself from fear
And once, I dreamt of putting all my eggs,
But one, into one basket –
Then awoke to the grey in the window
And felt the oval solid dissolve in my hand.
But this seems small knowledge to dredge
From so much turmoil, and I don't know
That I want to prove anything anyway.

[1962-66]

The Convalescent and the Mustard Field

Spring – my comforters said – Spring;
But they told me nothing of this,
This epaulette on the valley's shoulder,
This one yellow hill bedded in green
Softly plumped out with gold for a tired head.

Spring – they said, meaning what they meant,
But not this, this colour singing like a bird
Suspended in sunshine.

                    Spring – they insist, meaning
A sunny polishing of cars and progression –
Not this fully furnished golden barrow
Where I could lay down my pallor and fall
To sleeping clothed like a forgotten king.

[1962-66]

Fête

Only those people there are beautiful,
From each little life tethered to a chain
    Of the revolving chair-o-plane
They look down in silence at other people,
Or the suspended centre of their own being.
Other people resolving the annual loss
Of amusement, grip clouds of candy floss,
    Emerge red faced from animating
Their own drunken shadows on the bar tent,
Or stand half revealed against the night
Of mechanical music and barbecue light
    Like benign savages, well content.

Only those people in orbit are beautiful.
From their brief trance they do not cry,
But wistfully star the black depth of sky
    In one illuminated circle.
Beneath them, others release a beauty too
Where the damp grass is slowly worn away,
Until the green bruising offers a bouquet
To the night from the pestle of every heavy shoe.

[1962-66]

Goodnight

With you away, the traffic of the night increases.
    Someone, whose hands I do not know,
Guides a loaded lorry up the hill's black opposition
    With reason enough for wakefulness

And someone, somewhere, belts out a solitary life
    Astride the shindy of a motor-bike
Racing night to some desirable diminishing point.
    Nocturnal commerce is rife.

An owl hollows warm air in the empty lime tree avenue
    And forgetting the bloody mission,
I match his eyes with the luminous topaz of the moth
    Folded briefly on the wall to review

The problem of light before battering brilliant fate.
    And must get up, return wings to darkness,
Forget the pending spider, douse time prolonging light,
    And submit to night's limbless weight.

This morning an Indian announced himself at the door
    With cardboard case and curtain turban.
Glancing surreptitiously at my left hand, he offered
    Lovely ties from the portable store

And at the closing door offered, most anxiously,
    A journey, a long journey; or another
Gentleman perhaps. Yes, another gentleman perhaps
    And certainly a far reaching journey.

[1962-66]

Health

It hangs like bright fruit, just out of reach,
Growing in the window frame perhaps
Where boys flaunt their supple lives, toss caps,
Form knots of enviable fury, or screech
On skates, regardless of possibilities;
Where youths rev bikes ready to tear the green
You keep folded away, and the postman is seen
Delivering possible remedies.

130

Now the cat enters your room and passes by,
Or stops to knead your chest. She may come again
As if darkness did not matter, when you have lain
Too long awake and want to shout or cry.

Dust flours the bowl of flaccid grapes.
Sleep then, retreat to turn the dark leaves back
From other fruit. Reach, bite, make the kernel crack.
The deeper the sleep, the sweeter the fruit perhaps.

[1962-66]

My Aunt's House

The red brick burns and cools
In a spread of quietness,
And the windows steadily eye
The green and rise,
The grain and fall,
Of the field's fare
Overflowing the careless fence.

And above the slow undulations,
Minute and invisible birds
Continually engrave
The air and unguarded mind
With unfurling song,
So that rise of mist
And fall of dark
Cannot undo the pattern;
And I can fall asleep there
In a constant babble of larks.

[1962-66]

The Orangery

What pale gentleman with frilled wrists
Imagined these warm dimensions
And quizzed the bright trowels
Patting this afternoon into shape?

The little trees commemorate him,
Drinking from a tubful of earth
And offering whole armfuls
Of sentimental blossom and fruit.

If happiness were tangible,
Perhaps it would hang like this bright fruit
Ready to be taken from sombre leaves.
But it is not,and this fruit is not ours,

So we sit possessed, not possessing,
Married to these posed statues
Hewn from another landscape
And dragged to this conservation.

The blue uniform with folded arms
In the cool profiles and fruit
Keeps these clear windows for us,
On fictive blue waters and hot vines.

[1962-66]

Palmer: Cornfield in Moonlight

From the creased sides of the tree-thatched hills
I have watched seasons do and undo
Leaf, field, and distance, and thought I knew
All the lovely answers to the slow
Additions and subtractions of time.

132

But now, with your vision touching mine,
I am like Alice and can step through
The green reflection to the constant
Valley beyond, drenched with persistent
Moonlight and cold dew, where stubble
And sheaves glisten like honeysuckle,
Darkly shadowing the snail track path
And the nocturnal thanksgiving field.

I know the path and the distant bark
Of the fox from the hill wooded dark –
And streaming light strokes my borrowed hat.

[1962-66]

Roses Resist Night

Roses resist night with pale eloquence
Surviving dark tides that wash the house.
Beyond the window's narrow explanation
They take no light and their innocence
Rides moonless, but bright still with cool
Summer threading their accomplished shapes.
Starless, they find their destination.

Such simplicity dissolves the night;
But one pale head grown irresolute
Is marked for black experience,
When darkness floods taut veins, light
Dies from withering intuition –
And there is no quiet interleaving
Around one incorruptible essence.

[1962-66]

To an Unknown Poet
(for Donald Ward)

Involved as nameless flowers straining their sepals,
poems cram your pocket, or fall from your person
like straws from a flaxen fool and your eyes
brim with the distances you trek and reconnoitre.
But, without a huge and indelicate presumption,
how can you appraise the height of that bough
reserved for those who sing in unmistakable tones
stopping the paths of casual walkers?

Applauding hands and fusillades echo ceaselessly
from confusing rocks for all to hear, but their
origin is obscure and so, like Icarus, you are
always falling down the blue sky of your hopes.

Perhaps if you finally plunged the waiting sea,
a perilous descent would take you further than
an airy ascent made on unmelting wings
and you would surface hugging something ultimate
and cataclysmal as a Kraken, dredged from
livid despair and the hushed wreck of sunken lives.
Or you would emerge with an authentic mermaid
shaped beautifully as she whose form you pursue
relentlessly, her mouth a warm cave of pearls,
ready to be coaxed to that landing stage wedged
between stern rocks on the delectable and steady shore.

[1962-66]

Madame

Madame, the chaplets are withered from life,
the circlets bartered,
the crowns hoarded and unwinking.

Madame Recamier, Rome is bound in the dark bandeau
and the uninterrupted style
remains unattainable in time's acceleration.

Madame Abegg, danced with at a ball,
the music persists,
but the fans are folded and the skirts skimped.

Madame Blavatsky, all the cards are down
and the messages unaltered
in differently furnished apartments.

Madame, Madame, the blue skirts are unfathomable,
the smile indistinguishable
from its heavenly self, and the sky is the limit.

[March 1967]

Smiles

The possibility of smiles in the street below.
The silent parting of petals and small
Reflecting pools lodged in sleeping faces
Waiting beyond continual falls of dust and rain.

The descent to reconnoitre paving stones
To part the confusion of wet and dusty veils.
The oiled scissors waiting to flash,
The black bag empty and dragging.

Here cupboards are heavy with stale lace,
Portraits efface themselves, albums fade,
Mirrors empty and everything dies
This side of framed silver sheeting.

And after the dark descending flight, the act
Of pasting petals against night's hooded face.

[October 1967]

A Journey

On the line into the city
Someone has a regard for the journeying soul.
At one point a house facing the railway line
Displays a colossal text instructing travellers to
Prepare to meet God.

Sometimes my response to the size
And authority of the printed word is immediate
And I commence to consider ways of preparation,
Until I notice someone or something else –
A nun in my carriage staring in the opposite direction,
Or a linesman perhaps, with chocolate skin
And powder blue overalls painting swing lamp-posts silver.

If someone does not distract me from tentative preparation,
The long plunge into a black tunnel does not fail to do so.

[June 1968]

The Garden

On his drawing near,
The sun extends its terrible smile
And the roses lose their meaning.
All the saps and her blood
Cease their dark original coursing
When he, yet not he, draws near.
Soulless as a statue without eyes,
It is his broken outline only
Acquiescing wholly to insanity
Dressed in slippers and a linen coat
Offering her the awful weight
Of blind white hands.

[July 1968]

Boy Blue

Boy Blue, lift that horn,
There are other and darker landscapes.

The shadows in the meadows
Are not the shruggings
Of unaccountable beasts.

It is the open-handed wind
And soft nursery shapes
Waiting to eat from your hand
That move the grass.

Boy Blue, lift that horn,
Wake the blubbering dream from the corn
With bright gesticulation.

Do not make an issue
Of the colour of your suit.

[March 1969]

These Faces

These faces mouthing their black fruits
about my house.
Vinegar stains their lips,
salt crystallises their features.

Slowly they obliterate
paper and carpet patterns
until regular dimensions stand in danger.

They are not waiting for
sour wine in a tin cup
or a handful of ash.

It is the fondant-featured,
sustained in silver spandrels and glass,
who have devoured the apportioned honey.

The pot is scraped,
the cheap spoon bent.

[November 1969]

Diminuendo

My tiny niece, when taken to visit
The home of Wolfgang Amadeus Mozart,
Danced from room to dedicated room
Crying 'Where's Mozart, where's Mozart?'

The rapture of brief visits and brief lives.
Who would, with their finger at their lips
Hush such dancing to a hidden score
Or attempt concluding historical loves?

138

But when her dancing alters and slows to mine,
I may sidestep to tell her Mozart hated Salzburg
And how snow gathered for his funeral when he died.
Or she may improvise on this herself in time.

[March 1971]

birds

birds in the bush,
your song is indistinct
but clearly beautiful –
and you are about to take flight
before leaving a lasting impression.

bird in the hand,
your song is the morning voice
of sparring sparrows.
like municipal doves held to augur peace,
you will never take flight now.

[early 1970s]

Da Capo al Fine

That old Troll has lost his grip again –
Fallen headlong into the largest fjord
With the mountains' thinning mantles.
He'll surface again. He always does.
Rusty grievances and elemental cold
Revive him. Until then, there is time
For colourful openings and extended music.

Open the window, open the piano lid
And pick out a tune by our little composer
So that we are counterpart to all this.

Look, in the fjord below the steamer returns
Without having extended its repertoire
Of punctual notes; but it could arrive
At flashing music if, further on, a delegation
Waits to single out some expansive soul
From a cargo of printed and written matter.

No, don't close the window. Play Da Capo al fine.

[early 1970s]

Fortune

Misfortune, like fortune, wears its own crown.
The hydrocephalic prince is crammed
And beaten on the stairs for acting like a clown,

The haemophiliac cannot move beyond love,
The butcher's child still fattens on blood
When the bad-time slaughterers arrive

And the king tightens his reins in progress
Knowing his crown acknowledged, or run down,
Will be re-cast by heirs who digress.

Who find gold comfortable gear in the home.
Who support ten-gallon hats with ease.
Who robe supremacy in drab uniform.

[early 1970s]

140

Orford

The white owl flies his haunting garments
To and fro, to and fro,
Over the defenceless darkening meadow
As though coldness were something airy.

But it is cold; the growing dusk confirms it
And the two ladies on the road to the quay
Who will not relinquish Christmas, perpetuate it.
In their cottage window they still keep their
Decorative cardboard cottage roofed with woollen snow.
The little paper door, like the big wooden door,
Faces outwards, but neither door is an open invitation.
The faceless ladies sit with their backs to the window
Clenched around their essential heat like the
Neighbouring owl, whose familiarity they must know.

Now everything hardens and turns away –
But the boat sliding in from darkness
And the quayside dog, frantic with recognition,
Who runs to and fro, to and fro.

[early 1970s]

Sunday

Your heart is busy beneath my head
And a century away
My feet lie lost in the long grass.
Both shuttered eyes dissolve
The clouds and passing child,
But listening to the half spent day
I hear the crow that cracks the air with thirsty cries
And know she holds her blackness out above our heads.

The sheep, deceived, pull and tear
Near London herbage far from fields they knew
And the grass threading wind
Brings the noise of their persistent grief
With the children's clamour from the pond
Where wild boys are pendulum swung
From mild protesting trees.

[early 1970s]

Indris Lemur

If you can travel far by sea
Or tender intuition, you will
Find them clasping the high column
Of their last wooded sanctuary
Like some long-limbed angels.

Feature furred, yet ready to fly
Their endearing selves to different trees
For more endearments, fond solicitude
And necessary petals to live by,
To die by, in transcendent innocence.

So sensitive, a small bird can suddenly
Break the collaboration of their love,
Bruise them and leave their anxious eyes
Illuminating shadows endlessly
For indescribable consequences.

The honey of their inoffensive eyes
Is a new tributary to the soul.
They are the meek, tentatively on earth,
Inheritors of their inevitable qualities –
Released only in astonishing cries.

[mid 1970s]

Mother Goose: The Enchanted Garden
(for Maurice Ravel)

Even so, the garden remains.
The door in the impossible wall
Opens on to separate blades of grass
The silver timing of water
And effusion of tiny throats;
But the essential music is the silence
Occupying the arms of trees
And coiling in the circumference of petals.

All the fruits are imperishable
And none is allegorical.
Apples flush with innocence,
Pomegranates commit you to themselves,
Pumpkins lie where you want to be
And strawberries persist beneath snow
Collected in cool creases of warm
And perpetually flowering vistas.

The most tender nuance hovers,
Or passes, attached to transparent wings
And sometimes two indeterminate figures,
More than gossamer, less than their
Plausible selves, alter distances.
Nothing is asked of them, or you.
Serpents are lost brooches and as it was
At the beginning, it is again.

[mid 1970s]

143

Now

Now the sea pushes my thin door.
I can see it all from every window –
The constant changing of garments,
The consequential jewellery.

And if I look inwardly,
The windows continue their regard.
How loquacious and how like water
Is sheeted glass.

It informs the ceilings
Of different skies,
Blinds dry portraits,
Drowns fixed landscapes entirely.

And how like water is light,
Illuminating every voyage
Before embarked upon,
Whose incoming lifts me

Floatingly to high shelving,
From where I take a shell
And closely reassure my ear
Of land traffic's convoluted roar.

[mid 1970s]

A Secret

The cat is out of the bag
And the bag is seen to be empty,
But when the top is closed, promptly
It is filled with darkness – so

Now the cat has a life of its own
Roaming freely to and fro, to and fro,
And when it crosses anyone's path you know,
They pause to murmur 'puss, puss', bend low
And stroke it, down-a-down, compulsively.

[mid 1970s]

Skye Blue

Half way from the mainland
On the diamond water
To the aloof island,
Watch the unfurling blue
Flee from the ferry's foam
Through every probable mood to
The lovely rococo distance
In reiterating rain
And sun's bright persistence.

The blue rise and fall
In ranged mountains of the land,
Or island indistinguishable,
Throbs in the delighted eye
Rinsed in deep and dwindling waters,
Until gently intercepted by
A drifting cloud of rainbow,
The ghost of other qualities
Land lubbered long ago.

[mid 1970s]

Somewhere

When they call his name, he does not answer,
But they know he is hidden in the house
Storing total surprise in a dark cupboard,
Folding astonishment into heavy curtaining,
Or simply keeping a low profile somewhere,
Directing the dinky forces of floorway traffic.

Or he is in the garden, bright-eyed in brightness,
Beyond cultivation and green as grass –
While the sun shines.

So later they will open a door on dewy immensity,
Call his name again, and he will come –
Dark-eyed from darkness, his face white as a star.

[mid 1970s]

The Tapestry

No darkness, but the brightness of the first day.
Birds weaving the brightness, stitched on trees.
Trees already ripe with other colours
Storing, attainable syrups. Or simple trees
Filtering heaven with delicate complication.

Wide waters unfathomable with skittish monsters.
Or navigable blue scarves trailing silver shapes
Through hills and fields where strawberry leaves
And small flowers here, or there, propose a pattern
Mild herds and dawdling youth cannot trace.

No darkness, when sun and voices cram the hall
Or boys bring in fuel. But when these are gone,
Shadows quilt any meaning you thought you saw,
Obliterating towers, early horses and scarlet men,
Leaving presentiments of patient enemies in the bush,
The terrible agony in the wood.
Shadows sliding between you and every similarity –

Unless you recall the child in the blue lap of heaven,
The lattice of paradisal flowers.
But that was a picture seen somewhere else perhaps.

[mid 1970s]

Fireside Companions

The Furies are in the fireplace.
I have been expecting them
Since the cricket quit the hearth
When regular music was installed.

I hope they are cosy enough
And find me only briefly entertaining.
I hope too, the darkness in the house
Does not inspire them to sing
A chorus of formal disapproval.

Darkness is something the builder left.
They must know that – know too,
The red rug before them was set down
Without malice aforethought
And in deference to warm companionship.

[1977]

Only a Game

Now a dark green angel stands rooted
Somewhere in the garden's dark green trees
Silently observing a girl and two men
Who are playing skittles on flagstones of broad sunlight
Near a house that gently fumes its heart out to a summer sky.

A sombre thought is stirring in the angel's head,
And suddenly the girl looks up, shelters her eyes with one hand,
Sees, for a moment, the angel's green head, soft as a tree's crown,
And sees, quite clearly, beyond his elevated shoulders,
His half-opened wings, monumental as great sculpted yews.

Caught unawares, the angel swiftly blinds the girl
With the flashing light of his filtering garments –
And the girl closes her eyes, looks quickly away,
Looks to the game being fairly played out
On the flagstones of broad sunlight at her feet.

[late 1970s]

Coming Home

He will arrive later than the beginning
Of her prolonged anticipation,
When she has wrapped in blue for tiredness
And combed her pale hair from complication.
Her blood in his will leap to embrace itself,
Then recede to the new subtraction
More swiftly than her baffled heart can follow.

He will go after the brief satisfaction
Of greeting and few days altered loving
A little earlier than she expects,
Leaving her reducing time and his image
To small and simple prospects –
While unopposed dusk fades the furniture,
And only the balm and pale flame
Of the uninvolved white hyancinth
Illuminate the viewless window frame.

[late 1970s]

Angels I

Swedenborg saw three angels wearing hats,
Not one, but three simultaneously.
I have seen exquisite messengers from God
Drawn on ancient walls religiously,

Or flooding high windows with chromatic fire,
Or commiserating with the lonely
In the statuary of bereft suburbia –
But they were interpretations only.

I have seen a tailor's dummy in a window
Smiling benignly at two missing fingers
And have smelled flowers where there were none;
But no trick of falling light lingers

Long enough to misconstrue or reveal
Some divine presence to be wondered at,
Some presence to oppose marauding wrong at last
With, or without the most noticeable hat.

[1970s]

Angels II

Not that certain company of our other selves
Ready to return look for look upon reflection,
Familiar multiples with glassy features
Or low watery indistinctions.

150

Not even those selves trooping back again
Beautifully masked with fairy acumen
Glimpsed acting out our oldest and earliest
Gauzy loves against thinly painted trees.

No, those other selves – not awful visitations,
Woebegone doubles pierced with terrible eyes
Confronting us with the worst, the very worst –

Those assigned selves hovering beyond belief
Guarding us with immeasurable wings
Waiting for the quiet unfolding of our hearts
Petal by petal – those we can never again

Hopefully entertain with strained honey.

[1970s]

Ashridge

The trees insist on their dark shapes.
Darkness will not now drop imperceptible veils from the sky.
It is these commanding limbs and crouching greens that breed night.

Listen, a bird voice implores and drowns in the sombre depths.
How sadly the voice swims out over the hedged corn,
Like a tired attempt to attain a still warm beach.

Soon the colour of the willow herb will be uncertain
And the taste of wild raspberries will be an imagined red –
Unless we too, lift some bright illumination.

[1970s]

Fur Hat

How you go to my head
with your animal warmth
and aura of legends.

All summer long
I stroke your hibernation
in the dark cupboard

and then at the
drop of a leaf, I wear you
through the dwindling park

where wolves loosen wet tongues
behind sharpened trees
because of you.

In you I am clad against
military death in bitter pines
and the blue fingers of senility

and because of you
I wait for the great
white ache of sky to dissolve

blurring my vision.
O then I can queen the snow
in you and smallest boots

and watch someone signal
from the back of
the white-roofed bus

whose window frosted
with condensation rub clear
revealing.Argus eyes

as though Hans Anderson
pressed hot pennies on the glass
because of you.

[1970s]

152

La Belle à Bête

(for Maurice Ravel)

Beast is the hairy face
above the ornate collar,
the courtly air
nipped in the velvet waist
courting you.

Beast is the average beast,
not the other one,
the alphabetical arrangement
performing just so
in eiderdown.

Beast is the heavy weight
creasing your thin sleeve
leading you down the garden path
to indicate one rose,
the loveliest.

Your kind milk flows,
you turn your head
and the first blow falls
terminating the steady progress
towards the palace.

After the brief disturbance,
leaves subside
and silence widens
around your embroidered slipper
upturned in the cold grass.

[1970s]

Moorland

It is beginning to rain again.
You stand laughing by the river,
Tears in your eyes –
And the beery river rushes down
To me from you, wild with love.

I stand firm as a tripod
Long enough to take it all in,
But I am being washed away.
So much rain. So much love.

I keep the camera steady
Wondering what it will make of this
With only one rain-dimmed eye.

[1970s]

Moths

You have had your way at last
And we have taken to the jungle.
We spend every night on the verandah
Waiting for the appearance of stars
And for the great moth show to begin.
The pitched stars are always there,
But the moths have been waiting too,
Undisguised in the day's green curtaining.
See, when they come, the smallest fly
Airily as thought and the largest
Flap like damp umbrellas opening again.
Oh, we are all in a flap, for they are
Imaginably lovely, like painted angels,
And cannot be looked up in any book.
See, they are drawn irresistibly to
Our trim Tilley lamp of love.

Only the little yellow moth that comes
With Harmattan is missing –
But it will come, it will come,
Wearing its loose dusting of ground glass –
And we shall cover our nakedness and return home.

[1970s]

Negress

The negress sitting at the lighted window
Wears skin dark as the surrounding night
And she sits calmly in that skin.
The material she machines is endless and white
And every length is machined for the great
Hospital of the living and the dying
With the strength of her unhurried hands.
She will come to accept, without sighing,
The entire issue of the cotton mills.
Nothing distracts her, her head is low –
And she does not refer to night's insinuations
Beyond the measurement of her window.

[1970s]

A Night Out

Free at last! He slams the door,
Rides down the garden's darkness –
Until a shimmying shirt confronts him.
Quickly he pulls it from the line,
Quickly fulfils its drying shape.
How clothes make a man he thinks
And starts his white gesturing,
Whereupon the garden trembles,
Drops a leaf – and so it should.

156

Triumphantly he vaults the fence
Into the lane where, with more gesturing,
He scares a musical drunk dead sober,
Then, pausing, he remembers her –
Remembers her warm body, her cold rebuffs,
And returns to the garden in a fury,
Lifts to her lighted window,
Throws himself on a bedside chair.
She'll turn round soon and see
A crumpled garment resembling him
That is himself, and not be unmoved.

Feeling a cold entrance, she turns,
Lifts the personable shirt from the chair,
Laughingly shakes out wilfully assembled creases.

[1970s]

Portrait Gallery

He wore a pale rust coat,
almost pink in colour,
and a cap
pointed to match his fine nose.

His features were bird delicate
containing gentle tenacity
and almost pink in colour
with the branchings of fine veins.

From his greatcoat
his hand flowered perpetually
with a little paint brush
constant as an eleventh finger.

And leaning on the pavement
and hanging on the railings
were his fragile watercolours
all mostly pink in colour

with tangible dawns and sunsets
beyond fine branchings
of pale rust trees
bearing the finical weight of his art.

And beyond the railings
stood the art gallery
containing serious eyes of the famous
carefully varnished.

[1970s]

Saint Sebastian
(a watercolour by Odilon Redon)

His martyrdom is tied to a tree.
Pale as the back of a leaf, his body
Remains unbroken, but bends resignedly
As a leaf will under rain's white hammering –

Three Lilliputian arrows, finely drawn,
Contribute delicate woundings and at his feet
One lies fallen like an incredibly neat
Token of divine intervention.

And the tree. How blue the tree is –
A delphinium rod – a saturation
Of holidays after long reflection.
Mary, deeply concerned but calm, must be near.

158

Now only the limp flowers of his hands
Are lifted to heaven's bodiless air
Because assiduity has bound them there.
How sweet the dust of his bones will smell.

[1970s]

Proof Positive

No sleeper wakes in solitary bed
To find the flower plucked in a dream
Still held in the hand.

It is not for you to find in day's broad light
You are still wearing under plain clothes
The embroidered waistcoat you borrowed
To wear at yesterday's fête.
There is nothing hanging on the back of the chair.

But, come night, from the kitchen window
You may see a vine leaf shaking
In the wind of your shed light,
A rich hand held out to you from cold darkness.

[early 1980s]

Salomé

Papa Uncle I danced for you one, two, three,
Uncovered my face – now I find you niggardly.
Is one fat dish, one bloody severance
Too much to ask for my immortal dance?
You look like one who sees blood on the moon,
Yet this night's choreography is hardly done.
I shall follow my fame throughout Italy,
And as Patron of Art you can follow me.
I shall dance in the new white cathedrals of France,
Stand on my hands framed in stained brilliance
And take the plushy theatres of Europe by storm.
It will be art for art's sake – a matter of form.

[early 1980s]

Touring

We come to a legendary figure
Dividing the cold mountains
With the warmth of slow cattle,
Her blue coat diluted with weather,
White shouldered from the sun's yoke.

She conducts a rearrangement
And the velvet dignitaries batter
Sad confusion on the wet road.

I hate my smart shoes tucked
In the bonnet of our bossy black car.

[early 1980s]

160

Venice

Do not move another inch.
I have your weathered tiara focussed.
Do not sink on your knees under one
More onslaught of summery admiration
And do not advance the fee for
Sitting pretty in Saint Mark's Square,
Because I am coming, I am coming
For two winters. Yours and mine.

I am coming when the provoked Adriatic
Has wiped the fixed smile off the Lido,
When a raggy sky has washed the piazza tables,
When gondoliers steer, without interruption,
Wreathed fares to San Michele.

And do not sheet your empirical mirrors'
Dwindling dusks and riddled golds,
For I am coming by way of true awfulness
And the holiness of art to divine
The blue glass of ordered inwardness,
To draw all conclusions with long
Darkened reflections. Yours and mine.

[mid 1980s]

Muse

Something like you –
A classic profile,
A head wreathed with hair
And dark formal leaves,
Inclined always, to invisible music –
And dressed in falling folds,
Precise as marble.

Someone like you –
A still regarding face,
Lightly powdered,
Crowned with formal waves;
Someone chalky-handed,
Simply reading aloud,
Addressing wildest imagination.

Something, someone, like you.
But not in appearance.
Not in so many words.

[1980s]

Recording Angel

Understanding him to be remote,
Seated in remote azure
Wearing seamless white and wings,
Holding a gold plumey pen –
You discarded the thought.

But he is employed somewhere,
Straight and sober-suited,
Elevated in some high-rise.

And as, unhesitatingly, you
Reach for one more glass of wine,
He removes his pen from his breast pocket
And resumes writing in a lightly ruled book.

[1980s]

Thin Moon

A thin paper moon fading
With nothing at all written up.
Love will not come running now
Breathless with a torch of flowers.

Where lovers once dreamed awake,
Flowers lie pressed in unholy death –
Not that the river changed its course
To snare the city with rank remorse.

[1980s]

Spring Song of the Cleve Abbey Newt

The silver god has risen on the hill
        And runs down to the sea,
Runs cold as ice, but bears along with me.

A fat king with a feather in his hat
        Huffed one, two and three,
Blew down the stones and the brothers away
        Leaving only me.

Christ hangs broken upon the abbey gate
        And the silver god runs free
Through twice holy ground, fast enough for me.

[late 1980s]

Window

End of season, end of play – no one left
But a boy playing with the lonely sea
On the rain-wet shore below that runs
Helplessly on and on into advancing dusk.
Pushed under the cliff, houses look to themselves,
Look blindly away from the darkening game
In which the boy runs purposefully
Seawards and shorewards at the tide's edge
Like someone bearing a message no one
Wishes to receive – something written long ago
In his head, now overgrown with hair.
He never will stop running, for his limbs
Are oiled, his skill increases mysteriously
And the sea has become hopelessly attached.
When he runs shorewards feigning fear,
Like a father being chased by his own child,
The sea rushes after him, monstrously grey;
But when he turns, it whitens and retreats.

And while this goes on, here in the house –
As if by special arrangement –
Someone very quietly plays Reynaldo Hahn.
The boy does not know this; he is only human.
Soon the game must end unaccompanied.
But no, he is turning and running again
To hidden music, as if for the first time.

[1989]

164

Yes

Yes, like the passage of a bird that flies off course
Through an open window of the house –
And straight out through another open window;
Or a stone thrown at the sky-reflecting ocean
That bounces once, with a fountain-splash, before sinking.

And love for you certain, certain as the love
Of the winsome dog you once came across down an empty lane
That charged you from an unfenced garden, happily growling,
Its muzzle a black gloss clenched on a stone,
Knowing you alone could amuse, for ever – in passing.

[1990]

After Rain

Like a snail,
After long rain
You measure the garden path in silence.

The flowers have not changed place
There's nothing new, but familiar evening
And the immeasurable growth
Of another day darkly departing,
Coolly burdened,
Invisibly increasing everything still
With its fine presence.

[1991]

Drimindarrach

The deer are down the lane.
Darkening, they wear branches.
The trees, too, wear themselves with grace.

The deer have something to say.
One coughs; lets the matter drop –
And they drift down darkness to the loch.

Something barks now, untethered.
It is the deer saying something at last,
Roughly, simply. Stay now.

So far from home, so far,
And the ardent cat pinning you
To your rented bed in her tent of sloping roof.

[1991]

A Prayer for Sleep

Where is the angel who inhabits
The darker rafters of heaven?
When will he shake a wing
And descend carrying has fat jug?
I am caught, bent hopefully,
Like a woman at the hairdressers,
My head is low, very low
Waiting for the outpouring of darkness,
The beautiful alteration.
I am the felon, worshipping the block.

[May 1991]

Like Kylerhea

When I pass over to the other side,
I want the ferryman to wear
A blue woollen hat, a striped jersey
And canary-coloured waterproofs.
And half way over, where the narrow sea
Dissolves the narrow rain,
I want easy seals to rise
To the occasion of my passing
In their best black.

I want nothing of the far side,
Other than what is already there;
And when the ferryman says
'Nothing lasts for ever,'
I shall want to believe him.

[May 1991]

Edgar Allan Poe at Fordham

Hasten to Fordham.
Virginia lies dying
In winter's stricture.

Fuel for poems,
Fuel for stories, but no
Wood for the black stove.

A tortoiseshell cat
Lies curled on her riddled breast
Undertaking warmth.

An old army coat
Blankets her thinly against
Certain enemies.

He has placed the old coat there.
He has placed the small cat there.

[1992]

Index of titles and first lines
(titles are in italics, first lines in roman type)